Sometimes My Body Has a Mind of Its Own

Stories and Reflections on Living with Parkinson's Disease

Marc Sirinsky

HEVEL PUBLISHING, ASHLAND, OREGON

Sometimes My Body Has a Life of It's Own

Stories and Reflections on Living with Parkinson's Disease

by Marc Sirinsky

Published by Hevel Publishing, Ashland, Oregon

Book & Cover Design: Chris Molé, booksavvystudio.com

Photo of author hiking on Grizzly Peak in Oregon by Susan Glaser

Photo of author kayaking on the McKenzie River in Oregon by unknown

Library of Congress Control Number: 2021921590

ISBN: 979-8-9851271-0-2

First Edition

Printed in the United States of America

Dedicated to
the voice of exquisite silence.

קול דממה דקה

Contents

Foreword

I couldn't stop reading *Sometimes My Body Has a Mind of Its Own*. I enjoyed it so much that I read the entire thing in three sittings. The stories are short and compelling, the insights shine a light on what it's like to live and deal with Parkinson's, and the writing is conversational and intimate from start to finish.

The book is profound and there is no time wasted on puffing up the narrative with outside experts or fancy theories. Marc Sirinsky goes directly to the useful and compelling stuff. This is the deeply lived truth of one person. He shares a lot of wisdom in the stories, insights, and reflections.

"How do I find a way to function successfully in a body that is not currently able to do all that I ask? Is there a way to make peace with the body that I have and to stop feeling betrayed and distrustful of this amazing but fragile vessel that houses my soul?" These are the questions Marc addresses so beautifully. He truly walks the walk of how to live each day with wisdom and compassion, no matter what his body is experiencing.

I met Marc thirty-eight years ago in Southern California, when we were both volunteers at a fascinating workshop for teens and young adults on how to deal with racism, sexism, homophobia, and religious prejudice. Since then I've seen Marc wear many different hats. I went to his many theater performances when he helped adults with emotional and mental health challenges to use improvisational theater for healing and transforming their inner turmoil. I sat in on his innovative classes and weekly services at the progressive congregation he led for many years in Ashland, Oregon. I've watched his documentary films and seen his exquisite photographs, which celebrate the beauty and complexity others take for granted. And I have participated in hundreds of unguarded, honest conversations with Marc where we explored the pain and joy of being alive and being human.

What I didn't fully know about Marc until I read the manuscript of this book is that Marc is truly a gifted messenger for a crucial message we all need to hear right now—that our physical difficulties cannot fully stop us from being the persistent, creative, loving spirits that we know we can be.

His stories and insights in *Sometimes My Body Has a Mind of Its Own* contain important breakthroughs and wonderful creative tools for those who have Parkinson's Disease, and also for those who have other physical challenges. What makes his message so useful is that he doesn't write in a removed, clinical way. He passionately reveals his personal journey through PD as courageously as he used to maneuver a kayak through Class IV rapids.

As I read each story and insight in this inspiring book, I began to flash on various people in my life I would like to gift with a copy: my close friend from college who has had a longtime seizure disorder and yet somehow finds ways to make each day meaningful, creative, and loving; my therapy client with multiple sclerosis who has easy days and extremely difficult ones; several caregivers who will benefit enormously from understanding what works and what doesn't in helping someone retain independence and dignity, even when that person needs specific kinds of help on a daily basis. I'll definitely get a copy for a family member who has all sorts of physical challenges. She'll be able to use Marc's wisdom to maximize her health and joy, despite all that she has had to give up over the past few years.

I don't like books that over-promise or insist there is only one correct way. That's why I feel so thankful that Marc has created such a humble, realistic, one-step-at-a-time, non-preachy book on how to live fully with Parkinson's Disease and other chronic illnesses.

Please enjoy the experience of reading *Sometimes My Body Has a Mind of Its Own* and let it give you balance and support during the many moments when you or a loved one need them most.

~ LEONARD FELDER, Ph.D.
Los Angeles, March 7, 2021

Introduction

"All journeys have secret destinations of which the traveler is unaware."

~ Martin Buber

It was a little twitch, and it caught my attention. It was in my left upper arm. It was not painful. It was not irritating. Actually, it was mesmerizing.

Sometimes when I'm tired my eye gets a little twitch, but I've always thought that as soon as I got a good night's sleep it would go away. It always has.

But the twitch in my left upper arm wasn't going away, so after about nine months I thought it wise to check it out. My general practitioner wasn't alarmed, but after another three months it still wasn't going away, so I saw an orthopedic doctor who confirmed it was nothing to worry about.

I traveled to Costa Rica with good friends who are both doctors. After ten days of being with me, they, too, concluded it was nothing to worry about. Parkinson's Disease (PD) in its onset is like that. It's difficult to know what's just a twitch and what's a sign of something larger.

The twitch in my upper arm continued, but in addition, a twitch was developing in the fingers of my left hand, so I decided to see a neurologist. He recognized my problem immediately and told me, "You have Parkinson's Disease." Then he continued, "The good news is that it is not life threatening; rather, it's life altering."

Unknown to me, PD had been invisibly spreading its tenacious roots throughout my body for years. It has now been almost twenty years since my diagnosis, I am living consciously with PD, and I have a better understanding of the difference between life threatening and life altering.

Early on, I conceived of PD as an alien inhabiting my body. I saw it as something to be tamed. It was a cross between Jiminy Cricket and Darth Vader. Now I see it as part of me. It doesn't have a separate existence. And though it may be part of me, I still don't like it and I wish it would disappear.

This book explores some of the life-altering aspects of Parkinson's Disease and a variety of other physical challenges that happen unexpectedly to people. Each case exhibits unique characteristics in magnitude and scope. Some people have few symptoms, some have many. For some it progresses quickly; for others, quite slowly. For some it is life altering, while others seem to manage without too many adjustments.

I have learned the hard way that there is no easy path. For me, living with PD has taken intense determination and fortitude. Also, humor and lightness. And more than a little anger, depression, and inertia. No matter what I choose to do or not do, I now reckon with the idea that there are no guarantees. Life is neither good nor bad; life is just life and has aspects we do not choose.

I am on a major learning curve. Compared to the symptoms I have now, I didn't have much of anything in the beginning, but just receiving a diagnosis of PD set a whole series of thoughts in motion that took years to lasso and manage.

Back when I was first diagnosed, Parkinson's was primarily thought of as a degenerative movement disorder. Now it is acknowledged that PD works on many systems. Much current thinking suggests that it starts in the microbiome of the digestive system and moves out from there, affecting such things as mood, smell, taste, thinking, talking, sleeping, and sex. It affects how the brain coordinates the body's movements.

This book contains the kind of information I was unable to find in most other PD books. I tried to capture the spiritual as well as practical arts of living with PD and other challenging diagnoses. It is not intended to be a scientific look at Parkinson's Disease, nor is it a comprehensive story of my life and how I have lived with PD. It is an attempt to be something much smaller and much larger. It is my collection of reflections about things that have made my life a whole lot better, a whole lot worse, or both.

For the most part the reflections, which are based in my personal experiences, represent a way of thinking and living with challenges and adversity. They can be read not only by people with PD, but also by those with other challenges. These reflections are a call to myself to acknowledge what is true for me, and to differentiate that from what is just a dramatic story coming out of my mind.

My experiences have not always been pretty, comfortable, or optimistic. After years of trying to put a positive spin on things, I have learned there is much value in not sugar coating. Tell it like it is! Look at all of it—the good, the bad, and the ugly. I try to do that every day. Sometimes doing that helps to make the minutes and hours better. Other days are just plain hard, and watching my mind seems to do little or no good.

The reflections and the stories together are my attempt

to capture some of the highs and lows of what it is like to live with PD. No matter where one is on the continuum of symptoms, there are things that can be done to help.

This book is also for those who love people with PD and others with chronic conditions. I hope it provides a better sense of how PD affects real life. Just as it takes a village to raise a child, it takes a community to help one prosper with PD. I know this to be true, for I have seen it, felt it, and experienced it.

CHAPTER 1

In the Blink of an Eye

"You take whatever arises as your path to awakening. You don't wait around until the weather is better."
~Pema Chodron

Finding the right reading material for a trip is not always a trivial task for me, but some trips are no-brainers. I know just what I want to take—a book about the place I'm visiting, and either a novel or a collection of stories by someone who has lived there or that take place there. For most trips I also choose a self-help or spiritually expansive book, because being away from home and the known lends itself to breaking free of old patterns and behaviors. My reading choices open the window and hint at what I'd like to be thinking about during my travels.

I went through just such a selection process as I prepared for an eight-day kayak trip on the Main Salmon in Idaho. The book about the place would be T*he Main Salmon River Guide,* a US Forest Service Guidebook that describes the various rapids, landmarks, flora, and fauna, and includes history, legends, and tall tales of the area. That took care of the first two types of books I like to take. Two books in one takes up less room and weight. I trusted that the right self-help/spiritually expansive book would appear.

Books did appear, but with three days to go, none had moved to the top of the pile. Then a small, artfully designed booklet arrived in the mail, entitled *Dark Night of the Soul: The Journal of Hope* (healingenvironments.org). The title spoke to me.

During the previous year I had experienced my share of dark nights of the soul, and in going through those dark nights I had often arrived at a place of hope. This trip would be an excellent time to reflect on where I had been and where I wanted to go. I opened the well-designed booklet to see if it was indeed the right choice.

It began with a quote attributed to a person with the initials K.S.

> "All of us, at some time, pass through a dark night of the soul. Overwhelmed with pain and suffering, filled with fear and foreboding, we feel lost, hopeless, and abandoned. What is to be done? We may seek solace in nature, meaning in a spiritual quest, or guidance in practicing the presence of the divine."

Seeking solace in nature, looking for meaning in a trip. How perfect! I read on.

> "Above all, believer or nonbeliever, we may find relief in changing our relationship to pain. For suffering is increased by a lack of meaning. If we can come to accept that suffering is our teacher, not only unavoidable, but part of our path to growth, if we can accept this, the unbearable may become bearable. For it is through suffering that we become strong, wise, and compassionate."

Ding! I had found the right reading material. Or more precisely, it had found me.

I had already come a long way in my challenge to make peace with the pain and suffering brought on by a life-altering disease, but I knew that to embrace suffering as a teacher would be an ongoing spiritual challenge. On Thursday, with my quest for the right reading material complete, I packed a few extra pens and some blank paper in preparation for my Sunday departure.

However, the book spirits were not finished with me. The next night I was at a dinner for out-of-town friends and family of a couple who were to be married on Saturday night. I had been invited to the dinner since I was to be the officiating rabbi.

In preparing for the ceremony the previous week I had spoken on the phone with one of the guests, a man named Joel ben Izzy. Joel was a storyteller much admired by the two grooms, and we hit it off immediately. I had recently told one of his published stories as part of a teaching. At the time, I didn't know anything about him, nor did I know he was coming to Ashland, where I live. The Divine hand seemed to be actively at work.

During our conversation we discovered our paths had nearly crossed eighteen years earlier in Israel. We had worked at the same camp, doing the same job, one year apart. But what was most powerful was his personal story which, he told me, was soon to make its way to the shelves of bookstores and warehouses of Amazon.

Joel had been diagnosed with thyroid cancer five years earlier and had almost completely lost his voice. He had been reduced to whispering. His book is about his journey and how he grew from his pain and suffering.

Experimental surgery eventually provided an option,

although it was anything but a slam dunk. If the surgery worked, his doctor cautioned, he would get his voice back, but if it didn't, he would lose his ability to even whisper. What a choice for anyone to have to make! For a storyteller, it was akin to Russian roulette. Somewhat miraculously, the surgery worked.

As Joel told me his story, tears came to my eyes. I felt he was telling not only his story, but my story as well. This is a sign of a good storyteller.

I told him about my shock at learning I had Parkinson's Disease. How I had spoken during the Jewish New Year about the challenge of turning flaws into flowers, and how I hoped to learn the lessons of my challenges and to see them somehow as blessings. I hoped for an ending such as he had experienced, some new treatment that could make the disabilities of a progressive neurological disease go away.

I told him I would love to read his book. He had, in his motel room, an advance uncorrected proof which he said he would be happy to give me the next day at the ceremony. A bonus book for the river trip had arrived.

On Sunday, with the books and booklet all neatly packed in a blue dry bag, I began a series of flights that would eventually get me to Salmon, Idaho, the closest landing strip to the river put-in. As I made my way there, I began to feel increasingly apprehensive. I felt fortunate to have been invited, but I felt unsure of my place. This was primarily a group of experienced river friends and their families, people who had been guiding and dancing down rivers in kayaks and rafts for more than twenty-five years. I had been kayaking for six years and although I had navigated a number of class 3 and 4 rapids, I certainly didn't consider myself an expert.

I also hadn't had Parkinson's for most of that time. At least not that I was aware of.

On the flight from Boise to Salmon I was filled with awe. Lightning strikes in the past day had ignited a number of wildfires, and they were clearly visible from 9,000 feet in the air. Plumes of smoke drifted down rugged canyons seeking new pathways to carry their embers and ashes.

We landed late in the afternoon in a rainstorm. Friends of friends—people I did not know—met me at the airport and welcomed me like I was an old timer. We had our first group meeting at a Mexican cantina. After much laughter and too many chips, the eighteen of us set off for put-in, which I learned was still nearly two hours away down a washboard dirt road.

We hadn't been on this remote road more than twenty minutes when the smell of fire began to permeate the air. An ever-darkening haze of smoke obscured the blue sky, quickly turning into a thick fog. We stopped to talk to a ranger who told us that plans were to keep the river open, but a ten-mile section of river was closed to camping because of the fires. She cautioned us to be careful, reminding us we were going into true wilderness. I thought, *Where on this planet is it not true wilderness?*

The first of many group decisions was unanimous. We would not go further into the eye-tearing smoke but would return the next day in hopes that by then the smoke would have been chased away by a phantom wind.

Though we woke the next morning to a curtain of smoke, our spirits were in no way dampened. We stuck to our plan to go to put-in. After two hours getting there and three hours prepping the boats with gear, clothing, and food, we were on the river.

Days one and two were heavenly: morning wake-up calls to the blowing of a ram's horn, robust rapids, slow-moving sections of water perfect for interpersonal musings, hearty laughter, moose grazing by the river, delicious food, sandy beaches, star-filled skies, engaging conversations, wandering contemplations, kids playing joyfully together, old friends reconnecting, new friendships forming, and the delightful sound of voices, two guitars, a fiddle, and a harmonica.

Joel ben Izzy had started each chapter of his new book with a poignant and pithy wisdom story; I started each morning reading one of those tales aloud toward the end of breakfast. Discussions of what they meant could last a whole day.

Day three started and felt much like the others, only exponentially smokier. Today we would be passing through the section of river that was closed to camping because of the fires. By afternoon the smell of smoke stuck in our throats. Visibility was poor and an orange-red sun barely shone through dense haze. Each bend in the river held a mysterious and ominous allure.

At mile 79.2, we stopped at Bailey rapids, one of six rapids the guidebook recommends scouting. I'm always more nervous when a rapid has to be scouted, and this one was no different.

We all got out of our boats and tied them to rocks on the shore, then scrambled on the ankle-breakers to a better vantage point for seeing the dangers this rapid held for us. My more experienced companions offered valuable help in plotting my route.

As I made my way back from the scout to our boats, the

trip leader, who was scrambling just a few feet behind me on the unsteady river rocks, pointed out a rattlesnake. She wondered aloud if it might be an omen. I nervously replied, "It doesn't have to be a bad omen, does it? Perhaps it is a good one."

The expert kayakers, who knew how to glide down the river gracefully and effortlessly, took up safety positions in the calm eddies amidst the turbulent water to assure that anyone who got into trouble going through the rapid would receive the help that was needed.

Kayaking is as much a mental sport as a physical one. The intense focus and concentration it requires are deeply satisfying. The moment prior to entering a rapid is a moment of faith and surrender, a moment of trust and release. I know nothing else like it. I was the last to go and I focused all of my mental, physical, emotional, and spiritual energies on the task at hand.

I paddled well, following my line just as I had intended, moving between rocks and boulders, pushing through powerful hydraulic holes, crashing waves, and swiftly moving currents. As I passed the kayakers in their safety positions, they encouraged me on. I received a cheer at the end, as had every other member of our group as each raft or kayak made it through Bailey.

There was a great play wave at the bottom of the rapid where the other kayakers stopped to do tricks. From an eddy across the river, I watched with vicarious pleasure. The image of a yellow raft wrapped around a rock midway through the rapid caught my attention. I knew it was an illusion because we had just scouted the rapid. I paddled upstream to see what this mirage could be.

I had to get fairly close before I could ascertain that it was a large log shining golden in the light. I had been drawn to it by some kind of mysterious pull, but I didn't understand why.

Just then another party of boats on a guided trip started through the rapid one by one. First came an oar boat, then a paddle raft, a two-person inflatable kayak, then a bright yellow sit-on-top kayak. The sit-on-top was way out of line, heading directly for the 'golden' log. Before I could see the person clearly, the boat flipped.

The events of the next moments happened very quickly but will last a lifetime in my memory. The current pulled the man toward the log, where he became pinned. His life vest did its job admirably, holding his head above the rushing water. This couldn't last forever as the pressure of the water on his neck, head and body was intense.

In the instant it took to realize what was happening, the entire focus of everyone on the river shifted toward this man struggling for his life. I was closest to him and got to the river's edge first, but there was nothing I could do. His arms flailed for help. His eyes were looking toward another world.

Four expert kayakers from our group made it across the river in record time. By the time I scrambled up the large boulders to see what could be done, the man was no longer visible. The expert kayakers who had arrived on the scene were all well trained in river rescue. They hardly needed to talk to agree on a plan. They were in their zone.

Time was ticking. No one said it, but the last best hope was that the drowning man might be safe and alive in an air pocket. Miracles do happen.

The rescue attempt held its own real dangers. Someone would have to reach the log which was nearly mid-river to save the drowning man. The water that bridged the gap between the kayakers and the man pinned by the log was extremely gnarly and clearly something to be avoided. It wouldn't take much to pin another body against the fallen log.

The lead kayaker said what looked to me like a short private prayer and then made a leap from a boulder on the edge of the river to a smaller log that would serve as a stepping stone to the 'golden' log. The rescuer hugged the smaller log for his own life, half in, half out of the water. He pulled himself up onto the top of the log, stood, and carefully walked the tightrope of timber. The drowning man's life vest flushed off his body. Everyone watched helplessly as it washed down the rapid.

Not losing his composure the rescuer made his way to the big log where the man was pinned. The rescuer bent over and braced himself as best he could. He reached down into the treacherous water to grab hold of the man's arm. We all could tell from his sudden lack of urgency that the man was not going to be rescued alive. He was already lifeless.

The rescue operation turned into a recovery operation. Another kayaker made the leap over to the stepping stone log, then to the big log, hoping the strength of two might be enough to free the body of the dead man, but the power of the current pinning the man against the log was just too much. Using human power, ropes, vast numbers of carabiners and pulleys, a number of attempts were made to move the log and free the man's body. Nothing worked.

A voice played in my head. *You wondered why you were on this trip. Here's one reason. See who might need you. See if there are family or friends.* My clergy skills could not free the dead man, but I could help people facing a horrific trauma.

I spoke with the partner of the man who had attempted the rescue. A kayak instructor herself, she was in a state of disbelief. I said I felt that I should see if I could be with the family of the drowned man, if there was any. The idea seemed to surprise her. "What would you say?"

I didn't know what I would say. There was nothing that really could be said. But to reach out with love, sympathy, and comfort seemed like the right thing to do. She encouraged me to do what I needed to do. It was good advice.

I hesitated a couple of moments, fearing I might be perceived as an intruder, but then stumbled down the boulders towards the rafts of the guided trip where they had been secured in an eddy behind some rocks.

I was aware that my left arm was shaking more than usual. The tremor from Parkinson's gets accentuated under stress. In other situations I might have retreated out of embarrassment and self-consciousness, but in that moment, to be alive, with or without Parkinson's, was indeed a blessing.

It was a moment of a great paradigm shift in my own life. How silly to let my own sense of pride get in my way of being the best human being I could be at that or any moment. Tremor or no tremor, my humanness transcended any of my frailties or faults.

I asked a member of the guided group whether the drowned man had family or friends on the trip with him. I said I was clergy. He turned and looked in the direction of a raft with three people lying spent on the floor—the man's wife and his two teenage kids. "They are devout Mormons from Salt Lake City."

I made my way to their raft and identified myself as clergy. When they did not tell me to go away I received it as an opening, and I climbed aboard and sat with them, held them, cried with them, was silent with them, and offered to pray with them for what seemed an eternity. We talked a bit. They had questions, which they needed to voice. I felt there was very little I could do.

But having someone reach out to you at a time of loss can make a world of difference. Having someone expose and share personal vulnerability can give you the courage to embrace your own. Having someone help to hold you up can prevent you from sinking.

Opportunities to be supremely human happen every day:

- Drownings happen in the blink of an eye.
- Bike accidents happen in the blink of an eye.
- Car crashes happen in the blink of an eye.
- Heart attacks happen in the blink of an eye.
- A virus consumes the world in the blink of an eye.
- Death from a long illness happens in the blink of an eye.

Everything happens in the blink of an eye.

What would have been the foreground was the background as we left the scene of the drowning. Around the bend, wildfires burned from on high down to the edge of the river. Smoke and flames filled the air. We were too stunned to grasp the impact of what we were experiencing. Our altered state of consciousness was mirrored by the altered state of the environment.

When we arrived at our campsite, a couple of people approached me and asked if I would help our group process what we were experiencing. I had already begun thinking about it. Another rattlesnake was spotted and we talked about signs and omens as we prepared dinner. Someone noted that the smoke had entirely lifted from the area around Bailey at the time of the man's death.

After dinner we all gathered around the rafts. I spoke of how there were no rules for how to do what we needed to do. We had experienced something profound and intimate. Being present at a death always is.

We listened to the wail of a ram's horn. We talked about the life and death that was all around us. How the very fires that were burning and surrounding us were part of a cycle of death, rebirth, and renewal. Some shared other losses they had experienced. We agreed that the group that followed us had made a fatal error in not scouting or taking good safety precautions.

We prayed for the soul of the man who had died and spoke of how awake to life we were feeling, and how important it is to be mindful that life is lived at every blink of the eye. We did a spiritual cleansing ritual in the river, surrendering some of our grief to the flowing, living waters, and closed with an awareness and appreciation of the love and friendship that held us together. Spontaneously we began to sing a familiar tune:

Will the circle be unbroken
By and by, Lord, by and by?
There's a better home a-waiting
In the sky, Lord, in the sky.

We sang and sang, song after song, late into the night. Our trip had been radically altered by what we had experienced at Bailey Rapids. The river, like life, is filled with changes we don't plan for, wish for, or ever want to experience. Life flows in directions we never dream of, and therein lies a great challenge. When we are utterly flattened by the power of the river, by life, what does it take to get us to choose, as individuals and as a group, to get back into the flow?

We spent the next day at a beautiful beach. We lit candles and talked of rest and renewal, found our laughter again, and reclaimed the joy of being on the river. We saw bear, bighorn sheep, and mink. We scouted the rapids that called for scouting. And we safely ran rapid after rapid.

We continued to talk and heal. We still do.

What I learned on the river that day is that we are here to be the best human beings we can be, frailties, faults, and all. I learned the value of living life in the blink of an eye.

~

Reflections

How do we learn to live life when things happen to us and our loved ones in the blink of an eye? This question is never far from my mind no matter how well I am doing. The reflections on the next few pages look at some of the primary challenges of living with PD, such as tremors and other obstacles to communication in speech, writing, and typing. These are now at the core of my life.

Tremors don't go away just because I want them to. They are a telltale sign of PD. I can now recognize someone with PD a mile away. Before my diagnosis, I hardly knew it existed.

I have discovered ways to hold the tremor somewhat still for short periods of time. I find I can calm the tremor by very gently touching my index fingers together as though I were grounding electricity. The gentler the touch of the fingers, the more effective it is. It is not at all about holding still; it is about completing circuits. Trying to hold still only exacerbates the tremor.

When the tremor is doing its tremoring thing, no matter how much I try, I am not able to type or carry on a real conversation. The tremor takes a front seat and anything else I try to do becomes nearly impossible.

A tremor can range from a dull, incessant annoyance to an effective scene stealer, easily capturing the unwanted attention of an entire room filled with people. It is not so much a painful feeling but an exhausting presence of something that doesn't belong there. Sometimes it seems like my body has a mind of its own.

The meds are most effective for the middle two hours of each four-hour period, so the tremor usually appears in the hour right before I take my prescription meds and continues in the hour immediately following, until the drugs kick in enough to calm the tremor. It is best not to think of this as a time to accomplish much. It may be possible to read, listen to music, or watch TV or a film. The challenge of these activities is that they may put me to sleep and I'll miss the benefit of the two good hours when the meds are working efficiently, so I set an alarm, regardless of how tired I am.

Time. Where does it go? For much of my life I spent a good part of every day writing plays, films, television shows, sermons, or spiritual teachings. Even though I did many more things than write, I could usually find time to write each day. Now with all the things I do to try to stay ahead of the PD, I am fortunate to get in an hour of writing on any given day.

PD can easily become an exercise in managing time. More and more, dealing with PD has become a full-time job. Time disappears into constructing piles of meds and supplements I need to take at regular intervals.

Every day I take five prescription meds religiously every four hours. Before bed I take another five prescription meds. At each meal I take about twenty nutritional supplements. And if this isn't complicated enough, the prescription meds don't work well if they are taken within an hour before or after eating protein, which competes with the meds in getting through the brain barrier.

There are weekly appointments with doctors, healers, body workers, physical therapists, and trainers; monthly PD help groups; and a daily hour and a half for hikes. Like everyone else I need time to buy groceries, cook and prepare meals, and eat; time to read, pay bills, talk on the phone, and keep up with friends, all of which take longer due to my physical challenges. I also like to set aside daily time for meditation, prayer, and spiritual learning. And I need time to hold hands, talk with, kiss, and make love with my beloved. Did I mention time to write?

Speech is one of the most basic things we take for granted. It can be greatly affected by PD, at times causing me to stutter, slur my words, and talk at breakneck speed. These are all common to people with PD. It can be quite difficult to get started speaking, to say a word clearly or with enough amplitude to be heard by others, particularly if we are not sitting close to each other. That makes it even more important to speak clearly and with more volume. It is my responsibility to be heard. Not a day goes by that someone doesn't say, "Can you slow down?" or "Can you speak louder?"

It is not a done deal that people can't understand me. If I am mindful of saying all my words slowly and very clearly, people will be able to understand me. Speech is a great example of the fact that staying mindful can make a huge difference.

Handwriting and typing can be difficult as PD progresses. These days the tremor makes it nearly impossible for me to write by hand, or even to type. Well, I can write. I'm just not able to read what I write, no matter how hard I try. There was a long time in the early years of my PD when I was able to write, despite the tremor. My handwriting changed over the years. It gradually got smaller and smaller and more and more difficult to read.

At this time I can occasionally decipher a word or two that I've written, but it is not something I can count on. When I write a short shopping list, it is unreadable. I am unable to jot down a phone number, or appointment times in my calendar. I think I'll remember, but usually I don't.

I have discovered that my smart phone offers a couple of useful alternatives to writing or typing, but they're not always reliable. Dictating is sometimes a good solution, but not if I am slurring words or talking at breakneck speed. Dictation software sometimes makes unintended, and sometimes really wild choices for me, and then I can't even remember what I originally intended to write. One time I wrote the words "I love you," but because I spelled the word "love" as "l-u-v," the software picked it up as "lust." It's a good thing I caught that one. My friend would have been quite surprised to receive such a message from me!

Tapping a physical or virtual keyboard works sometimes, but not when a tremor is very active. It's a challenge to make corrections. Trying to type with a shaking arm and hand can lead to serious consequences. I have sometimes activated multiple purchases online with mouse clicks that I could not stop. Before I knew it, the damage had been done.

CHAPTER 2

Freezing in L.A.

"It's only our mistakes that bring us to the place where we should have been all along."

~PICO IYER

WHEN I WAS LIVING IN SOUTHERN CALIFORNIA, a friend of mine asked how she could help me deal with the challenges that come with Parkinson's Disease. Since I am male, my first reaction was, "I don't need any help." But since I was also a relatively young male humbled by Parkinson's Disease, I decided to tell her about "freezing." Freezing is a strange thing to talk about in Los Angeles, where in mid-March it gets a bit cool at night, but not cold, certainly not cold enough to freeze anything. The freezing I am talking about can take place anywhere, any time, and has nothing to do with the weather.

Freezing is a bizarre and mysterious involuntary phenomenon that happens to many with PD. When freezing, one becomes totally stuck in place, unable to lift either leg from the ground, unable to safely walk even an inch. When this happens to me, attempts to move sometimes bring on unbelievable leg shakes. Other times there is no perceivable movement. The simple act of approaching a doorway can trigger a freeze. It doesn't matter if the door is open or closed, or even if there is no door at all. A doorway is sufficient. Following behind someone makes it worse.

Sometimes I must shed good etiquette and plunge through a door first. I have asked strangers from a distance to please hold a door open for me so I can enter a store. Sometimes getting a moving start from afar can make a difference. Other times the moving start turns into a freeze. I become like a pillar of salt, as if I didn't have enough faith to get me through the doorway. Stress plays a role, but not always.

I can sometimes tell that a freeze is coming on because my gait becomes more awkward and each step takes considerably more effort. I have devised some helpful tricks to use when I find myself freezing or frozen. For example, one trick involves carrying a short walking stick and kicking it with each step forward, which can also be effective at preventing a freeze from happening. Sometimes these tricks work, but sometimes they don't. They may be little more than smoke and mirrors, but we all like being seduced by smoke and mirrors. That's what magic tricks are all about.

This freezing isn't just strange and a nuisance. It is both of those, and more. In trying to move forward with my feet anchored firmly by what feels like a concrete block, my torso falls forward. I lose my balance and am unable to do anything to minimize the effects of the fall. So far I have hurt only my pride, but freezing can lead to when hips can get broken.

I had just moved to L.A., the city of the automobile, without one. I had wheels, but they belonged to an odd-looking folding electric bicycle. I'd found a tiny secluded studio apartment situated above a garage to call home. I called it my Paris flat, for if I imagined being in Paris, its tiny size seemed apropos. It felt romantic and spacious.

In this sprawling city of spacious living, I shifted perspectives quickly, one minute feeling like an expat living abroad, the next feeling like I was back in college. In both scenarios I was intent on being independent.

It was my first full day in my new home. There were some items I wanted immediately. Bins for socks and underwear, a few kitchen items, and some hooks and hangers. Nothing very special. Just basics.

I mapped out a bike route to a store that would have everything I wanted. It was 3.6 miles away, on the other side of the San Diego Freeway. I brought rope to tie the bins to the front and rear racks on the bike.

The route worked fine until I encountered one hitch—construction. There seemed to be road construction everywhere. The sidewalk going under the freeway was closed. I could legally and most safely retrace my steps about half a mile to a traffic light, or I could cross Wilshire Boulevard right where I was.

A small raised median strip separated the eastbound and westbound lanes. I figured I could do half the road at a time, using the median strip as an eddy, a safe place to pause and get my bearings, before scouting and doing the second half.

When I lived in L.A. a few decades ago, I would have done this without a second thought. But on this excursion I had second, even third thoughts, about trying to move safely in a place that was inherently filled with danger. If I froze crossing either half, I would be mincemeat. I couldn't think about what might happen because just thinking about it could raise my stress level, and raising my stress level could trigger a freeze.

I felt no signs of an impending freeze, so I made my move and quickly got myself and my bike up on the median strip. Before even catching my breath, I noticed a good clean opening on the second half of the wide roadway. I went for it and felt a rush of adrenaline.

How best to describe this? In the language of kayaking, it felt like I was crossing a Class III rapids. Class V is the highest, and such a rating would signal extreme, life-threatening danger. This Class III crossing felt entirely manageable and contained just enough thrill. Mumbling a prayer of gratitude, I stepped onto the sidewalk on the opposite side.

The remainder of the ride to the store needs no description, except to say that traffic was heavy and seemed a tad hostile. But I was happy to be outdoors and on my own, so I did not let that disturb me.

At the store, the department I was looking for was right inside the door, and I found everything on my list in record time. My only real decision was whether to buy one or two of the three-drawer bins. They were big and bulky, not making for easy bicycle transport.

Because everything had gone so well up to that point, I decided to test my tie-down skills. River rafters carry all kinds of shapes and sizes of cargo, and each item, no matter how awkward, needs to be tied down well in the event of a flip that might land it all in the water. Though I knew it would be wiser to get the two bins another time, when I had a friend with a car, I liked that I was getting to practice my rafting and kayaking skills.

If there had been a video surveillance camera on the sidewalk where I struggled to attach the bins to the bike, someone would have seen some hilarious footage. My tie-down skills were not up to snuff after all. I'd been amusing myself for about half an hour when a man on a bike stopped next to me. He amiably commented, "I've carried a lot of strange loads on my bike, but this is up there with the best of them. Would you like a hand?" I said I would happily accept all the help he could give. I even offered to assist *him*.

The good Samaritan's intentions were welcome, but the two of us were a modern incarnation of Laurel and Hardy. We finally called it quits. The two bins were attached well enough for me to walk the bike home gingerly, but certainly not securely enough for me to ride.

My meds were beginning to wear off, moving would soon become difficult, and I was eager to get on my way before I ran into trouble. I was hot, I hadn't drunk water or eaten in a while, and I was feeling both literally and emotionally shaky. I saw all the tell-tale signs of danger accumulating like a snowball rolling downhill, gathering size and speed.

My mind was dulled by dehydration and hunger. Staggering down the sidewalk filled with pretty people, I was afraid if I stopped moving or tried to enter a store to get a drink, I would freeze, so I swallowed my meds dry.

I made it to within half a mile of my new home when I froze at an intersection. After three signal changes I knew I was in trouble. I was frozen at the edge of the road. Traffic was increasing. The street began to look more dangerous, more like a Class IV rapids. Crossing the street looked potentially life threatening. This was not good.

I was so close to home, but so far away. I knew enough to stop, to call it quits on this foolish stunt. I called my friend to take her up on her offer of help. My window of opportunity to do a self-rescue had passed, and I asked her to drive over and toss me a throw rope.

I sat on the curb and waited patiently, keeping an eye on the food store parking lot across the street, where she would leave her car. People passed by and glared at my loaded-up bicycle. They had every reason to assume I was a new face among the local homeless population, carrying all my belongings wherever I went. I did nothing to indicate they were wrong.

When my friend drove into the parking lot I felt an enormous sense of relief, and waved my hands in the air so she could spot me. My fear immediately receded.

I had devised a rescue plan, but first we had to unload the cargo from my bicycle. She untied the cobweb of rope that loosely held the two bins to my bike racks, carried them across the street one at a time, and loaded them into her car.

Next she removed the bags that hung from my handle bars, as well as some other small bags and the oversized bag containing the three drawers, from where they were hanging behind the seat and took them to join the bins now stowed in the trunk of her car. Then she took my bike across.

There was finally only one thing left to get across—me. She gave me some water and an energy bar, and we waited through at least three more signal changes.

I still could not get myself started, but then I remembered a trick that sometimes helps people to get unfrozen. I said, "Draw an imaginary line with your foot in front of my feet and tell me to step over the line you have drawn." She looked at me with disbelief, for the first time seriously entertaining the idea that I might have been hallucinating or was in some way mentally impaired.

I told her again, emphatically, to draw an imaginary

line. This time she played along and drew the imaginary line with her foot. "Now tell me to step over it." The light had just turned to Walk.

"Step over the line," she said. I did.

I had an impulse to jump up and down and cheer, but I wanted to take no chance of doing anything that might reactivate the freeze. Nobody has ever crossed a road so intently. As quickly as I'd become frozen earlier, I had become unfrozen.

With that obstacle out of the way, I became more aware of my body again. I could feel the meds kicking in. My energy returned as the nutrients and water rushed through my body like internal rapids on a river, and I felt invigorated. I felt it was important to get right back on the horse, and was sure I could ride myself back to my Parisian flat. My friend watched as I confidently mounted my bike and rode off toward home. We both arrived safely at my flat a few minutes later.

My friend said to me, "When I was in Vietnam, people rode bikes piled high with stuff. But they knew what they were doing. Don't do something stupid like that again. There are plenty of people who would be happy to help you out and take you shopping." I knew she was right. I also knew that my desire for independence sometimes gets in my way.

I amused myself that evening thinking about what I had attempted to do. I didn't know whether it was good or bad that I hadn't taken a picture of my loaded bike. I'd considered it, but I didn't want to have to rub my nose in it later.

I realized I could live in LA, but not as I did twenty years ago, and not as I did pre-PD. I was learning that my stubbornness could get in the way of making wise decisions. I was also learning that too little dopamine could get in the way of making wise decisions.

Reflections

Sometimes I move too fast. Sometimes I move too little. Sometimes I don't have the flexibility I'd like to have. The challenge is not to be constricted by the PD. The following reflections look at different ways I move my body and parts of my body.

Wheelchairs, walkers, canes, and walking sticks all have their time and place in life with PD. Sometimes they can help promote mobility and balance, but can be misused as well. Having grown dependent on them long before that dependence was necessary, I realized how easily they could become crutches.

I used a wheelchair for a number of months. I have used canes and walking sticks on and off for long and short periods of time. They come and go. I have come to see that it takes courage to set them aside when I no longer need them, and it takes courage to use them when I do.

There are many paradoxes about living with PD. Whatever aid I end up using at any given time, I try to remember, and to remind others, that these items do not enable me to walk, but rather, they enable me to initiate movement. They make me more secure and may help me avoid falling.

When someone offers a hand, it is a kind gesture, but actually it puts more pressure on me to move forward. The problem is not that I can't stand up. The problem is initiating movement, and there is little anyone can do physically to help with that.

When I have not been able to stand up on my own two feet and walk without danger, I have really appreciated how awesome legs are. I have come to see how fear of falling sometimes results in not going anywhere without a stick or cane. Sometimes I have left the house without a walking stick, then gone back for one because my anxiety sets in. Sometimes getting the stick into the car is enough to ease my mind. At the other extreme I can sometimes run when I cannot walk.

I discovered this while hiking in my local mountains. My walking seemed ungraceful, and I remembered how in high school I had loved long-distance running, which uses a very different set of muscles. I decided to try running on the trails, thinking it would be either one of the smartest things I'd ever done, or one of the stupidest. Lo and behold, I was able to run, and I felt elated at this discovery.

I have continued running, and I still feel elated every time. I know it sounds difficult to believe, but even running can be an option when I can't walk as gracefully as I'd like.

I often don't use it for walking. Bears and cougars have been sighted in the local mountains. I carry the walking stick should I have to defend myself. So far that has not been necessary.

I have found another use for the 'stick.' It is a perfect size for twirling like a baton. I walk and twirl. I am working out new moves all the time. Little did I think PD would lead to a baton twirling routine but it has. If you should bump into me on a trail one day and I have my walking stick with me, ask to see my routine. It should be good for a laugh.

CHAPTER 3

Double Manna

"In every walk with nature one receives far more than one seeks."

~John Muir

IT WOULD BE ALL TOO EASY TO SUBMIT to the urge to stop moving, which tempts me often. PD works not only on a physical level, but also permeates the mental, spiritual, and emotional levels. To keep up my walking is an important daily challenge. To stay ahead of my illness, ordinary walking is not enough. The brain is soothed not simply by strolling, but by highly aerobic hiking, walking with a purpose and a pace.

Even though I know that to be true and I am committed to a daily hike almost as a spiritual practice, the PD holds me stationary with a subversive coating of tacky glue, like fly paper. Much of each day is spent knowing I have to get out of the house and get moving, really moving. But it takes so much concerted effort to move that an entire day can be spent not moving.

In summer I have the excuse that it is too darn hot, so I wait till the end of the day, that time between sunset and nightfall, when the air begins to cool. Fully aware of the consequences of giving in to my sluggish self, I know I must not fold. In a burst of energy, like a booster rocket lifting a space capsule into orbit, I get my act together and sneak in a walk, just as time and light are running out.

I'm lucky I live near a trail called White Rabbit. It's three miles up steep switchbacks and three miles back down—more than a hill but not quite a mountain. It is not actually remote, but it feels remote because the steepness keeps most people away. It always feels like I've accomplished something worthwhile when, out of breath, I make it to the large rocks at the top. They are a good place to rest, drink some water, and look at the view that includes two dormant volcanoes. At the top, dripping in sweat, I feel ten steps ahead of the PD. I try to remember that feeling the next day when lethargy once again attempts to keep me at home.

Each summer day I repeat the same pattern, finally bolting into action as the moon becomes visible. The ascent makes my heart pound and takes my breath away. But the descent is actually the more difficult and treacherous activity, especially at dusk. The steepness, loose soil, protruding rocks, and gnarly tree roots all conspire, singly and in unison, to knock me off my feet and tumble me down. Getting off the mountain in one piece demands good balance, quick reactions, and faith in the agility of my body.

Faith in my body is something that PD tries to steal from me, but faith is the safest way down the mountain. I can't be overly cautious, because that would invite a fall. I do best when I momentarily surrender my balance but then safely recover without fully falling. It's like a kind of dance. This is where faith comes into play. Not the faith that God will intervene and prevent an accident, but faith in my body to do exactly what it needs to do to stay upright.

As almost any serious athlete can attest, repeated stress causes premature signs of wear and tear on the body. For me, continued hiking on steep inclines has produced similar signs of wear and tear, especially on the knees. The pain I was beginning to feel after each day's exercise was starting to serve as a new excuse to remain still. The voice of the PD gained an unexpected ally. One day it got so bad that I could not take even one more step without excruciating, debilitating pain. Hiking was out of the question. To grin and bear it was no longer possible.

It took visits to an urgent care facility, to my regular doctor, and to an orthopedic surgeon to make it clear that I needed knee surgery. Three weeks later, a torn meniscus was shaved down so it would stop getting caught and pinched. After a month of twice-weekly physical therapy successfully improved the muscle tone, I resumed hiking, but it took about two weeks to work my way up to the mid-point on the White Rabbit trail. That was far enough. By the time I returned home my legs were shaking from exertion, almost in synchrony with my arm tremors.

Soon it was late fall, early winter. Heat could no longer serve as a delaying tactic, but nature kindly provided another excuse. In the Pacific Northwest it was now rain that offered me an out. I had to organize my bursts of energy, faith, and trust during the times when it was gray and chilly but not wet.

Not feeling quite as agile on a post-surgical knee, I took to hiking with a pair of walking sticks, which gave me additional confidence by providing balance. They also engaged my arms and upper body in rhythmic movement that prevented my arm tremors from gaining the upper hand, and took some of the pressure off my knee in the steep descents.

Wanting to avoid dependence on the walking sticks to reduce the arm tremors, I took to using a Thera-Band, a stretchy rubber exercise band. I stretch it every which way and it gives my upper body a needed workout as my legs keep up a challenging pace on the ground.

The downside of a Thera-Band is that stretching it out in front of me might make me appear to be a menacing strangler seeking prey on the trail. So as not to scare anyone, especially a solitary woman, I stop stretching my Thera-Band when approaching a fellow hiker. I can only hope this makes me appear less threatening.

On one particular day, neither brighter nor grayer than the ten preceding it, I was hiking without poles and decided to go a little further than I had since my knee surgery. As I pushed forward I could feel my legs getting tired, and a hint of the shaking that comes from over-exertion. It didn't seem wise to overdo it.

I was on a side trail that ran parallel to and just above the main trail. I could see the main trail, it wasn't far away, so I decided to cut over. The terrain between the two was rough, and my confidence that I could recover if I slipped was not high. With about five yards to go—a rather steep five yards—I froze.

I froze because I had temporarily lost my faith and trust in my agility to navigate the drop-off safely. Shuffling and taking small steps didn't work and I could see that it would result in a certain fall. To move forward with confidence was no longer a realistic possibility. I could not pick up either foot to attempt to move forward. I was precariously stuck and began to shake.

Two women were briskly approaching down the main trail. When I'm alone I let myself shake spastically, but when someone is watching, I do my best to suppress or camouflage it. I wanted to stop the shaking so the women wouldn't notice me. A small tree beside me gave me the impression that perhaps I was partially hidden. But I couldn't stop shaking, and they saw me. My cover was blown. They stopped and asked if I was okay, to which I replied that I would be okay when I got down from this ledge, but until then I was not okay. They asked how they could help.

One of them was using walking sticks, and I asked if I could borrow them. She promptly handed them to me. I explained that I had Parkinson's Disease and was frozen. My challenge was not hiking; my challenge was initiating a movement, taking a first step.

"The temptation is to try and help me down. It doesn't work that way," I told them. "But if you draw a line in front of me with your foot, and tell me to step over the line, that usually does the trick."

They looked at each other, then me, to see if I was for real. "Do it," I encouraged them. "Draw an imaginary line with your foot." One of them took the dare. "And now you have to tell me to step over it."

"Step over it," she said. And without any Herculean effort, I picked up one foot, then the other, and, using the poles to support myself for additional balance, I was down on the main trail in seconds.

"Wow!" they said together, as if on cue.

"I'll be fine now," I assured them. "Sometimes it's just hard getting started. I can get going now because it's flat here." I could tell they didn't totally believe me, and I may not have totally believed myself, either.

"If you're okay with it," they said, "we'd like to follow you and make sure you get back safely."

I knew I should be able to get back safely, but my confidence had been temporarily shattered and I sensed these were not two women, but rather two angels sent to protect me. Indeed, I felt comforted by the idea of someone or something watching over me. So I said, "That would be greatly appreciated. It's very thoughtful of you."

They playfully warned, "You'll just have to put up with our gossiping."

Without missing a beat, I replied, "No, I won't. I have an iPod. I'll just put on my headphones and listen to music, and you can gossip your hearts out."

They laughed. I put on my headphones and turned on my iPod. I started walking briskly, as if to prove to them I was just fine, and they followed me, gossiping the whole way, about a mile and a half. At times I was tempted to turn off my iPod and see what they were so deliciously chatting about, but it didn't seem right, so I didn't.

When I got back to the fence where the trail begins, I stopped and waited to thank them again for following me. I wanted to tell them they were angels, but angels, I think, prefer to work incognito.

As I walked the rest of the way home via paved streets, I thought of a series of photographs that would be interesting—photos of people who stop to help me when they see something is not right. I imagine in a few years I'd have quite a number of photographs of strangers who have stopped to help me, my own personal deck of Angel Cards.

~

Reflections

The one central element that underlies everything else in this book is the need to move—the need to move my body, increase my heart rate, and be outside in nature.

Hiking is a joy. I love pushing myself to go faster uphill. I listen to some of my favorite songs on an old iPod and my iPhone counts my steps and distance.

The forest is ever-changing. I look forward to each day's experience and what I might see that I have never seen before. Oh wait, that's not entirely true. I hope I don't see the cougars and black bear that share the woods and trails I hike five days a week.

Hiking regularly has made me feel remarkably less diseased. I've been telling friends and family that I feel the best I have felt since my diagnosis almost twenty years ago. People see me and notice a difference. Two years ago I was using a wheelchair, and now I'm literally running up and down steep trails.

Balance is really important. Falls can result in broken hips. Broken hips as we age can often be the first step leading to a last step.

I've been doing nearly daily hikes with a friend, and we have on occasion gone off trail and bushwhacked our way through steep forest. During the winter months we sometimes need to climb over fallen trees. They are slippery, even icy, and I have fallen a number of times. I don't think much of it because I blame it on the ice. My hiking partner doesn't see it quite that way. She feels I'm putting us both at risk, and not looking closely enough at the dangers of my limitations. I contend that these slips, these falls, can happen to anyone, and do not necessarily reflect the effects of PD on me.

I see my stance as a way to show myself and others that I am successfully fighting the effects of PD. My friend believes I am in denial, that there are less dangerous ways for me to fight those same effects.

In deference to my friend I'm now asking myself, When is a slip not really a slip? It is an uncomfortable question, but I need to continually ask it. I try to be on the lookout for situations when I am denying what I really know to be true. Every time I slip and fall again, the questions must be asked once more. When is a slip not really a slip? When is a fall not really a fall?

Balance comes up in other ways, too. I have always walked a bit funny. I'm constantly losing my balance, then catching it before I fall to the ground. But I trust myself to succeed. I believe my sense of balance is very good, and that is what keeps me upright. To some it may look rather precarious. I start to fall, I catch myself. I start to fall, I catch myself. It works for me.

Actually, this is what we all do when we walk. We switch our weight from one side to the other. We surrender the illusion of safety that comes with standing on two feet and learn how to dance our balance and imbalance together.

If I can manage to be playful and inventive when feeling stuck, I have a better chance of moving forward. This is particularly true when I run, and it becomes more like a dance. I follow my legs and my legs follow me. Neither one of us is completely in charge, but we both desire to work together, and for the most part we do.

I am cheered not only by how well this works, but also by the fact that my playfulness is the vehicle for discovery. When unable to walk forward, I've tried dancing sideways or backwards. Sometimes I think I have struck gold.

Smart watches—my Apple watch—is my new best friend. It identifies when I fall and checks with me to see if I do or do not need help. If I do not respond that I don't need help, it will call in my location to emergency services. An amusing thing happens when I fall—my watch taps me to see if I'm okay. For a moment I'm more concerned about responding to my watch than I am about checking to see if I'm really okay.

My smart watch also monitors my heartbeat and is able to tell when I am becoming anxious. I play a game with this application. I try to notice my anxiety and subdue it before the watch gets me to do the same thing. I used to use medication to calm the anxiety. Now I use the watch.

Another essential use of the smart watch is its ability to remind me to take my medications. It can tap me on the wrist so I can use it anywhere without having to disturb people with the alarm. Combining the eating protocol and the medication protocol can be complicated, so it's helpful to not have to think about it. The watch can take care of it.

It's good to look for new solutions to old problems. There are new gadgets coming into the marketplace all the time.

Some might, intentionally or unintentionally, have a feature that will be helpful with PD. I now do a variety of different breathing exercises and/or meditations with apps on my watch to calm my anxiety.

Daily exercise was never a central part of my life. Six years ago I was nearly dragged by a friend to an exercise class for people with PD. The body that's reacting to PD does not want to exercise so I repeatedly have to break through that same inertia. I tell you this because I am now fully committed to the value of exercising.

Over months I increased exercising from one day a week to five or six days a week. Soon I was able to walk and hike again without any major difficulties.

I have slowly learned that exercise is a key component to keeping me active and mobile. Some say it is as important as the meds. I think they work in tandem; I can't see one without the other.

Recent studies confirm that one to two hours every day of highly aerobic activity keep the degenerative effects of the disease in check. Of course there are no guarantees, but the positive difference it makes in my life is unmistakable.

The exercise class gradually woke me to the realization that I didn't have to be a victim. It didn't happen overnight; the change took place over many months. But one by one I began to reclaim aspects of my life I had turned over to PD. Inch by inch, row by row, I saw my garden grow.

There are now specially designed PD classes featuring various types of exercise, including riding stationary tandem bicycles, hip-hop dancing, non-contact boxing, spin classes, ping pong, hopscotch, jump rope, swimming, t'ai chi, ballet, and yoga classes. The list grows longer each day.

People who have PD can do many proactive things to improve their quality of life, and I have tried many, even ones like boxing that I'd never imagined myself doing. My body responds well to each with their unique challenges.

Just a few days without exercising can make a huge difference in my life, and so I try to work through any resistance that prevents me from doing what I know needs to be done. I cannot say enough about the importance of exercise.

CHAPTER 4

Travels with PD

"We may run, walk, stumble, drive, or fly, but let us never lose sight of the reason for the journey, or miss a chance to see a rainbow on the way."

~ Gloria Gaither

After my elderly parents moved to Palm Springs, California, I thought it would be easier for me to go visit them than for them to come to me. Considering the way my journey unfolded, I'm not entirely sure that was an accurate assumption.

My brother-in-law printed my boarding pass and I was delightfully surprised when it said, "Pre-checked by TSA." He explained it meant I wouldn't have to take off my shoes or jacket, open my bags for inspection, or take out liquids. As he said, "It takes the stress out of airports."

My anxiety about traveling in public with PD was almost always enough to kick the tremors into high gear, but knowing I had TSA clearance, I arrived at the airport feeling pretty on top of my game that day. I wasn't actually a hundred percent "normal," but I was able to walk freely without fear of freezing and/or shuffling instead of truly walking. The line at the pre-approved security checkpoint was empty, so in a bold move, I went for it, eschewing the wheelchair I had requested. I reasoned that it would be a good confidence booster to travel without wheelchair or special assistance. I haven't done that in maybe five years.

I took advantage of being an early boarder because of the PD, and was able to put my bag in the overhead without having to wrestle for space. My seat was on the aisle, two rows behind first class, and an attractive young African-American woman sat down next to me. She looked to be in her late twenties, wearing stylishly ripped jeans. We said hi, then she quickly pulled out her phone and earbuds and divorced herself from any interactions with me.

When we took off it was fast approaching the bewitching hour at the end of my med cycle, a time of transition, discomfort, and increased symptoms. Since the flight was only about an hour, I figured if I took the next round of meds right at the beginning of the flight, they should kick in for walking purposes just in time to help me get off the plane.

My seat neighbor discreetly watched me shaking as I tried to manipulate my water bottle and plastic pill container without dropping anything. I decided she seemed open enough for me to ask her to please hold my open water bottle while I put the pills in my mouth. It was clear why I was asking for her help—the shakes—so I didn't feel it was necessary to explain my condition.

I downed my PD meds in one fell swoop, wondering if they would kick in before the plane landed. I have learned I can 90 percent count on the drugs working in about an hour, but there is that 10 percent wild card, so I took another swallow of water and downed a small dose of Xanax—a benzodiazepine that calms the central nervous system—because I was feeling pretty anxious.

My seat neighbor and I went back to our chosen solo activities, she to music and games on her smart phone, I to music and meditation. I watched myself as if from a balcony in a theatre, separate from myself. The shakes lessened and increased, lessened and increased, and for a while I watched myself ebb and flow into and out of near panic-attack mode.

My heart raced. My breath became shallow. I was glad I had begun to learn to push through the tough transition hour, to do whatever was needed to carry me through the discomfort of waiting for the meds to kick in to an adequate level. I could do things but it was difficult, like doing everything inside a giant bowl of thick pudding.

At the top of my anxiety list was a fear of freezing under the duress of needing to exit the plane in a timely manner, and navigate the narrow aisles and exit door. All had been trouble spots for me at one time or another in my many years of PD. I am feeling more and more that this strange disease is almost entirely in my head, and I felt that if I didn't freeze from the stress, I would be okay.

I decided it would be prudent to ask for assistance in case I froze or had other PD symptoms getting off the plane. It seemed wise to at least make someone aware of what might happen to me, rather than risk people projecting onto me their own ideas of what they saw. My seat neighbor seemed like the logical person to ask, but she was in dreamland so I hesitated to disturb her.

The flight attendant came by for final safety checks shortly before arrival and presented my lucky moment. My neighbor's seat was in the reclining position and the attendant tapped her shoulder, asking her to move her seat into upright position for landing.

After giving her a chance to respond, I asked my seat neighbor if she would be willing to help me in getting off the plane, adding that of course she was free to decline. I explained that I have Parkinson's, that the challenge with PD is often initiating movement, and that once I'm in motion I can walk for miles. I told her I probably wouldn't freeze, but asked that if I did, could she please draw an imaginary line with her foot in front of my feet and tell me to step over the line. It was an odd request to have to make of a stranger minutes before arrival at our destination, but she didn't hesitate and said, "Sure."

When I thanked her for being so gracious and open, she responded, "We're all here to help each other. We all have something."

When the plane landed I told her I was feeling good and would probably be fine. She said, "It's okay, I know what to do." I stood and moved into the aisle near the front of the plane with my carry-on in my hand. No long line of passengers itching to get off had yet developed. It was a very good opportunity for me to safely deplane. So I went for it. Step after step. I just kept going because I could.

The only real challenge that remained would be if I stopped and couldn't re-initiate movement. I briefly turned around a couple of times to see if my angel was visible so I could thank her. I didn't see her, and knowing that stopping could put me at risk, I kept moving, choosing steps over an escalator.

Then I came to my all-time airport nemesis, a revolving door—a real-time torture chamber for people who freeze in doorways. If I were to freeze inside one of the sealed pie slices, I would make quite a spectacle of myself. They are equipped with emergency turn-off switches, but if I were frozen, I wouldn't be able to get to the switch.

The longer I hesitated, the harder it would be to go inside. To this former kayaker, it felt like being thrust into a Class V rapid on a rapidly moving river. I saw little choice. I took a deep breath and entered the turbulent waters.

While I was caught in its clutches, I could see through the glass my mom and dad waiting for me. Their faces lit up as they saw me emerge. They didn't know how relieved I was to feel safe again. I hugged both of them.

While my dad paid for the parking at a machine nearby, I kept an eye out for my angel. I waited a few more minutes and saw a couple other people who had been on the flight, but it was time for us to leave. Waiting any longer would have made my dad more impatient. His parking ticket had just been paid for, and now the clock was ticking. I had to relinquish the idea of giving my thanks to the young woman who had made this aging, ailing man feel a little less alone in the world during a challenging ten or fifteen minutes of his life.

So wherever you are, thank you, and I hope you know what a difference your openness and kindness meant to me that morning. Bless you.

~

Reflections

PD is a humbling disease. We are all vulnerable creatures, but what is unique for people who have externally manifested physical disabilities like PD is that we are not able to hide our vulnerability. It is there for everyone to see. Having always been a somewhat shy person, I don't like people to see my mistakes or shortcomings. PD strips away the ability to hide. I can't even hide from myself.

Some of the things I find most embarrassing are:

- **Drooling** without cause as my sweetheart and I are about to kiss. Need I say more?
- **Drooping mouth** is what it's called when I find myself staring at whatever I happen to be looking at with my mouth open. It is an inefficient way to breathe and it looks rather stupid. I put an index card on my bathroom mirror that says, "Do your best to avoid getting into bad habits." It's a good reminder not to let the PD take charge.
- **Bad posture** is a challenge because the PD is trying its darndest to make me hunch over and slump. It wants to turn me into a slouching rock. I do my best to stop it now, rather than waiting until it is a lot more difficult.
- **Tricks** are coping mechanisms, playful ways of holding the PD temporarily at bay. PD can throw curve balls at me, and I need to stand in the batter's box and respond to each pitch. In football terms I need to feint right while "the guy with the ball" (my PD) goes left. Tricks are my creative solutions for dealing with the cards

I have been dealt which includes Parkinson's Disease.

- **Resting Tremor** refers to the nature of the PD tremor. This means that the tremor can disappear when that body part is being used. The tremor will most likely reappear when that body part is at rest, relaxing or sleeping.
- Though it can be difficult to be playful in the midst of a tremor, playfulness is the best way to discover tricks that might work. Getting more and more anxious doesn't help; it only makes things worse.

  As in football or maneuvering rapids in a kayak, the same trick won't work every time, so it's good to have a backup handy and ready to go.

Here are some tricks I use for dealing with tremors or a freeze.

- *Hard candy or chewing gum.* These work great in trying to lessen a jaw tremor.
- *Music.* I use a pair of earbuds to listen to music while I walk. It can make all the difference in the world in terms of walking comfortably. The music gives me a rhythm and a pace so I don't have to focus so much on walking. I can just focus on the music.
- *Busy hands.* Because tremors are lessened when the body is moving, one way to suppress a tremor is to move my fingers using things such as prayer beads, malas, and worry beads. People often think I'm doing a spiritual practice when I am using them. Maybe it brings out the guru in me.

- *Laser lights.* A small red laser light, often used as a cat toy or to bring viewers' attention in a slide show, is useful for me when I have a freeze. I point the laser light at the ground and try to step on the red spot. Then I move the light in the direction I am headed. I step on the spot and continue in this way for as long as is necessary.
- *Molasses.* Sometimes I imagine walking through a tub of thick molasses. I move forward by lifting one foot and then the other up out of the sticky mess. It's a bit like snowshoeing in heavy, wet snow.
- *Walking stick.* I hold the stick in my hand and kick the lower part. It gets me started moving, then I continue to kick the stick, alternating between my right foot and my left. This can actually get to be fun. It sometimes makes people watching me laugh out loud. They are usually not laughing at me, but with me.
- *Drawing a line for myself.* After I told my Buddhist therapist about ways she could help me break a freeze if I needed it, she came up with a question for me. "Would it work if you made a recording of yourself on your cell phone and told yourself to draw a line with your foot and then step over it?" I tried it the next time I froze, and it actually worked!
- *Ice skating.* Recently I was cleaning out my garage when I came across an exercise gimmick adapted from furniture movers—plastic circles about ten inches in diameter that slide across floors. They are used like ice skates—instead of lifting up your feet, you slide them

forward. In a freeze, sliding doesn't seem to go by the same rules as walking. This is a great trick I use in the middle of the night to get to the bathroom. I keep the circles right next to my bed.

- *Crawling.* This is sometimes the only option. I can crawl when I have to move and can't walk. It's not my favorite option and in some circumstances can be risky, but sometimes when I have to do something like get to a toilet, I do what I have to do. Crawl. It can be tough on the knees, depending how far I need to go, but it gets me there, and it sure beats the alternative. It can feel mighty humbling.

Go with the flow. Sometimes a trick stops being effective. I find it's helpful to be flexible and stay open to discovering new tricks. The David Bowie song "Changes" reminds me that what works today probably won't work tomorrow, or some other tomorrow. Everything is always changing. I've had to get used to change. Whether it's things I am unable to do any longer or medicines that stop working, I must never assume I have the full picture. It's a drag, but the greatest teacher in my life might very well be the thing I most want to disappear—PD.

One promising change is the way researchers are now looking at the possible origin of PD. It was thought that the brain has a primary role, but now researchers are finding that the brain plays second fiddle to the gut in this condition. What was considered a movement disorder is coming to be thought of as a gut disorder. It may take a long time for gut disease to be accepted as a primary cause.

- **Use it or lose it**. There are a number of activities in the category of use it or lose it. One is the voice. If I don't project my voice and exercise my vocal cords, I will begin to speak far too softly. I remember the "Low Talker" episode on the Seinfeld series. It's worth watching on You Tube because it's funny, but it also illustrates how speaking too softly can create a big obstacle in communication. I had to stop seeing a friend who has PD because it was too frustrating to not be able to hear her. Asking her to speak up seemed to do no good at all. There are now machines you can type into that will project a voice, but obviously there is a lag time and it's far less satisfying to have an exchange of ideas.

Which leads to my next entry in the use-it-or-lose-it category: Typing. If I want to keep typing, I need to keep typing. It is the only way to keep fingers nimble and moving well enough. During a tremor, not being able to maintain control of the fingers might lead to another typing challenge—sometimes I cannot stop from tapping on the keyboard. I have no ability to control the incessant tapping, which also interferes when I'm using my cell phone. At times it appears that I am trying to stab the life out of my cell phone with my finger. Sometimes I worry that the number of strong and excessive tappings is going to break the glass screen.

Another area that fits this category is sex. The tremor is distracting and makes it hard for me to focus on the pleasure at hand. Someone once suggested to me that my tremor could be like a great vibrator to use on myself or my partner. I did not find that to be true. The tremor is a distraction and the distraction may not go away, so I need to choose how much I want to have sex. If it is important to me, I must find a way to keep it up despite the distractions. It can be done. It is also worth noting that the physical act of sex releases dopamine into the brain. It is a rare example of PD doing something beneficial. So get that dopamine flowing!

CHAPTER 5

Time to Go

"I must be willing to give up what I am in order to become what I will be."

~ALBERT EINSTEIN

IT HAD BEEN TWO YEARS since I'd spent much time on the river, and I was determined to get back into a hardshell kayak. Nothing can make me feel so at one with the river as being alone in a vessel gliding gracefully through the water. It is not still water that I seek to cut through, but white water rapids, where Zen meets the thrill of adrenaline and the two carry me deep into my aquatic amphibian roots.

I'd been in Bali for five months and was almost at the end of my stay when I learned there was a perfect river for me to paddle—a fun and forgiving Class III river. The water level had just risen high enough to be paddled. I was determined to have the experience of kayaking in Bali. After putting out an all-points bulletin for a hardshell kayak, I had begun to accept that such a vessel did not now exist on this island. An inflatable kayak or a raft, which they did have, would not do.

Two weeks passed and my return date was fast approaching. The call of the river helped me make peace with the fact that although I hadn't found a hardshell, the joy of being on the river could still be experienced in a less worthy vessel. I chose an inflatable kayak.

Yudhi was my driver of choice in Bali when I needed to get somewhere beyond walking distance. Over the duration of my stay he showed increasing sensitivity and concern for my personal safety, especially when I was trying to cross busy streets. He would actually stop traffic for me so in case I froze, I wouldn't be hit by a car. No one stops traffic for anyone in Bali.

Since Yudhi had become more friend than driver, I invited him to join me on the river. He accepted. It would be a treat for him, a thank-you gift for all he had done for me during my time in Bali, while also fulfilling a self-serving piece for me—my safety. If I shook, appeared rigid, walked oddly, or stared vacantly with my mouth drooping wide open, Yudhi could explain it to the river guides sensitively, straightforwardly, and concisely in Indonesian. It would be reassuring to have Yudhi along.

On the day of the river trip I tried to time my meds to avoid lag time between cycles. I was doing my best to make a tenuous situation less likely to blow up in my face. I was nervous and excited, and those two emotional states tend to make the meds less effective.

After paying and putting clothes, cell phone, and valuables in a locker, we boarded a shuttle bus for a short ride to the boat put-in. The atmosphere amped up significantly. Busloads of rafters arrived and were divided and placed with a guide. Yudhi and I were the only kayakers, and having paid considerably more to kayak than to raft, we were afforded the royal treatment. We were whisked though lines and received our life vests, helmets, and paddles in record time.

The equipment was sufficient, but nowhere near my familiar state-of-the-art gear. The vest was bulky and not ergonomically designed; it felt more like a straitjacket. The paddle was heavy, unfeathered (both blades parallel to the water surface, which is more challenging for me), and way too long. The helmet was fine.

The organizer's call to keep things moving had the reverse effect on me. I had just signed my waiver/safety release and was feeling glad that no symptoms had yet become so evident that they would decide I was a safety risk and not take me. Unfortunately, Yudhi didn't realize how tenuous the situation was, and he went ahead of me. I froze.

With a multitude of eager, testosterone-charged rafters surrounding me, I, the inflatable kayaker, froze. I tried to break it but knew if I rushed, I might fall. I shuffled a few steps forward like a drunk. People were noticing. I was afraid if I didn't pull it together quickly, I might be discovered as a customer too disabled to be taken on the river.

I stood my ground, took a deep breath, and focused all my attention on initiating a step. I knew if I could take one, the rest would follow. And then, in a miraculous moment of synergy, the motor skills clicked into sync with the correct neurological processes, and one step led into another. I made my way down approximately 950 steep and uneven rock steps to the river. My legs and brain did not desert me, and I arrived safely at the narrow put-in, the place where we would enter the river.

The rafts quickly filled and people were given the most basic of instructions before their launch. Their spirits seemed more attuned to boarding an amusement park ride than getting ready to raft safely down a turbulent river.

I wanted to say to our two guides, "If I shake, it isn't because I am nervous. I know what I am doing. I have been a Class III hardshell kayaker for many years. The shaking is because of Parkinson's Disease." I thought it would be important for our guides to know of my condition before we took off.

Yudhi smiled at me and said he had just told the guides about my PD in Indonesian. The guides were fine with it. They explained that it was standard operating procedure in the narrow top section for guest and guide to go together in the boat, and Yudhi reassured me it was not because I had PD. When we met up with the main tributary of the Ayung River, I was welcome to paddle the boat by myself.

As it turned out I was grateful, as rocks and quick turns punctuated the Class III whitewater. This was not the kind of rapid to build up confidence after a two-year absence from paddling.

The upper section was fun and immediately connected me with what I so love about rivers. The guide was true to his word and good at what he did. As soon as we got to the main section of river, he said the boat was all mine if I wanted it. I jumped at the chance.

A few moments later I moved toward the rear of the inflatable kayak as my guide dove into the river and swam over to Yudhi and his guide in the other kayak. It was quite a contrast. The three of them on top of each other in one kayak, and me all by myself in the other.

I was in heaven, alone in a kayak on a challenging yet safe section of river in the jungles of Bali. I paddled with gusto and confidence, wanting to give assurance to the guides that I did know what I was doing. They saw that I could read the river well and they relaxed. They kicked back in their crowded boat and enjoyed what appeared to be an easy morning for them.

Then I started getting tired. I could feel the difference between the state-of-the-art, high-tech, lightweight paddle I had at home in the United States and this monster. I could feel the weakness of my body, my strength diminished from more than twelve years of deterioration. I knew at any moment I could be in real danger. I recognized the signs.

I looked to my guide on the other side of the river. The sound of the rapids was too much to talk or shout over. I tried to signal him that I wanted him back in the boat with me. At first he didn't understand what I wanted. When he got it he slipped over the side of his craft and went into action.

I had just barely enough strength to paddle hard enough to propel myself out of the main current into calmer water behind a large rock to wait for him. That gave him a fighting chance to get to my boat before I began drifting into the top of the next rocky rapid. He made it in time, but not by much.

He didn't want me to paddle. He told me to just rest. It was at that moment that I looked up at the beautiful jungle ravine that held the jewel of a river and said to myself, *This is my last river trip. I cannot safely take care of myself. It is not okay to put my life in the hands of someone else, or to risk another's life. I have seen someone die on the river, so I know those things happen.*

As I had these thoughts, tears came to my eyes, tears of joy, tears of sorrow. My tears fell down my face and a few fell into the river. It was a mixing of the bitter with the sweet. My guide took me down the rest of the river safely, and I was so grateful.

I feel grateful to all those who have taught me how to read a river, how to love a river, and how to be safe on the river. It has been a wonderful ride.

The river will always be in my mind and in my heart. As Michelle Shocked sings in her song of the same title, "The secret to a long life is knowing when it's time to go."

It is time to go from the white water. Adios, or as they say in Bali, *Selamat jalan.*

Reflections

When I was in graduate school as a writer and director in Theater Arts, one of my teachers said the best thing a student can do to be a better writer/director is to travel and see how other people live, work, and play.

I've come to realize there is another aspect of traveling, physically or virtually, for a person with PD—seeing how people treat their maladies and diseases, and how they heal. Some approaches may appear alien or primitive, and some may appear highly technical. It's important to remember that just because something seems primitive doesn't make it ineffective.

The unfortunate thing is that there's no approach that can encompass all healing paths. I had to piece together my own healing system by going to a number of different practitioners—naturopaths, neurologists, Chinese doctors, shamans, Feldenkrais practitioners, and so on. I need to be in charge of my own healing and decide what is best for me and what I want to try. I also need to remember no modality comes with guarantees.

In the United States health care system only a few specified modalities are covered by health insurance, and not everyone is fortunate enough to have even that. Other forms of treatment are considered bonuses. That is, I can use them if I can afford them. If the covered options serve me best in dealing with my PD, I'm all set. Otherwise the financial challenge can result in missed opportunities.

I sometimes find myself confused about the effects of each modality and the interrelationship among the different modalities. For example, when I consider adding various supplements that the functional doctor recommends, I need to understand how, and if, they will interact with the meds my neurologist prescribes.

I was determined to heal from the effects of the PD and knew I wouldn't be satisfied solely with pharmaceuticals. The neurologist told me that at best, medications would only treat the symptoms, and I wanted to do better than that. I looked around and didn't find too many alternative treatments, but I knew in my heart I had to keep looking.

It's a strange word, "degenerative." It doesn't leave room to heal. So when I heard about **Yin Tui Na,** a new protocol developed by the Parkinson's Recovery Project, I signed on the dotted line.

The acupuncturist who developed the protocol, Janice Walton-Hadlock, has written more than a thousand pages of information about PD, its symptoms, and the effects of the medications. She has made her book, *Recovery from Parkinson's Disease: A Practitioner's Handbook*, available to anyone who wanted to read it.

I ordered the material and when it arrived, promptly devoured it. This doctor really understands the complexities of PD far more than most doctors do. It's rumored that she herself had PD, which may explain why she seems to understand the disorder from the inside.

In short, her protocol is based on a type of Chinese medicine practice called *Yin Tui Na*. Walton-Hadlock has a unique theory that PD comes from a childhood foot injury that never healed. She believes that *chi* (life force energy)—which normally travels down the torso into the legs, then into the feet, and eventually into the ground—is blocked as a result of the childhood injury to the foot. The *chi* cannot pass down through the foot so it reverses itself, travels upward, and gets released through the extremities in a tremor. The *Yin Tui Na* treatment is intended to make the foot feel safe enough to release the blockage and allow the *chi* energy to pass through the foot and into the ground.

It appears to be an amazingly simple practice. A person who is sensitive to working with *chi* energy holds the foot with two hands, allowing it to feel safe and embraced. Each session lasts about an hour. The process requires a great deal of faith because there isn't much to see. The treatment is very subtle. I had seen big changes occur from subtle procedures, and I wanted to believe it would happen with this work.

Following it would require that I be off my medications during treatments. The two systems were not compatible, and it would be dangerous to use both at once. Walton-Hadlock couldn't say how long the treatments would go on, and she let me know the whole journey would be very demanding.

I would also need to see her three times per year at her office in Santa Cruz, California. The rest of the time I would need to have someone practice *Yin Tui Na* on me locally. A friend could practice the treatment on me, but she would need to come to be trained. I was fortunate enough to have a very good friend who said she and her husband would be glad to go with me to Santa Cruz. We all took this practice very seriously, for if it could truly lead to recovery, I wanted to give myself every chance in the world for it to work.

I started receiving the treatments and at the same time, slowly worked my way off medications, which was not easy. The tremors got worse. Not taking any meds showed me how devastating the disease could be. At some point I would need to figure out how much I was willing to suffer to stick with a protocol I wasn't sure would get me anywhere.

About two years into the protocol, Dr. Walton-Hadlock told me that it would get even worse, much worse, before it got better. She said that I was not even in the "hell" period yet. It was discouraging to me that I still hadn't made it to hell with two years of practice behind me and no recovery in sight.

I did what I'd hoped never to have to do: I abandoned the protocol—and my hopes for recovery—and went back on meds. The quality of life that I got from using the meds seemed worth the trade-off, but it was a sad day and I grieved the loss of that hope.

Feldenkrais practice was recommended to me by a physical therapist. Like *Yin Tui Na*, it is a gentle practice.

Moshe Feldenkrais's revolutionary approach integrates scientific insights with practical ways to help people. It involves both body work and corresponding physical exercises to retrain the neurology of the brain. The man was years ahead of his time.

I began to work with a local Feldenkrais practitioner who introduced me to the world of "neuroplasticity."

Neuroplasticity enables the brain to compensate when damage occurs. It is the capacity of the brain to reorganize itself by forming new pathways and connections throughout an individual's lifetime.

When Feldenkrais first introduced the concept of neuroplasticity, neurologists deemed it to be New Age gobbledegook. Brain doctors and researchers now acknowledge that the concept of neuroplasticity provides us with an essential understanding of the mysteries of the brain.

Harvard-based neurologist Norman Doidge has written two books on neuroplasticity and is credited with popularizing the concept. In *The Brain's Way of Healing,* Doidge devoted a whole chapter to the work of Feldenkrais and wrote this about him:

> "Genius, of the magnitude possessed by Moshe Feldenkrais, defies categorization...He could function at the highest level in nuclear physics, as a martial artist, as an inventor, as a developer of top secret counterespionage projects, and as one of the most prescient observers of neuroscience."

After I read Doidge's book, I upped my sessions to two a week. I felt I was on the cutting edge of Parkinson's treatment. I still do. Feldenkrais is my longest continuous practice and I find this subtle work to be quite effective. For example, I can walk into a session moving with difficulty and by the end of the session my mobility has improved and I am moving more gracefully. I think anyone who'd like to move better with PD would be wise to explore the work of Moshe Feldenkrais.

Shiatsu, commonly known as acupressure, was suggested to me by a dear friend who found it helpful for Lyme disease. The practitioner who worked on me understood the meridian lines of the body and figured out ways to eliminate the tremor by a method very similar to acupuncture, but without needles. This quickly became one of my best practices to eliminate or minimize symptoms.

Functional Medicine takes a holistic approach to health—it looks at the whole body as one system and works to understand the underlying causes of a disease. Understanding a patient's unique lifestyle, genetic, and biochemical factors provides a blueprint to the functional medicine practitioner, which is then used to try to get the body to repair itself by giving it whatever help it needs. In my case this includes supplementing any vitamins and minerals my body is lacking, either because I don't produce enough or my body isn't using them properly.

The challenging part of functional medicine is that it works slowly and sometimes I find it difficult to be patient. It's like the turtle in "The Tortoise and the Hare." It can take a long time and demands a lot of faith, but for my situation it has been helpful.

Do I think the functional medicine approach could work independently of the neurologist and prescription medications? No, I don't. Our bodies are complex. I think each of these practices plays a role in their synergistic effects. While I have greatly benefited from some of the alternative forms of practice I've used, I do believe that without the foundation of the mainstream medical approach, I would not have made as much progress toward recovery.

CHAPTER 6

Delivery

"The cave you fear to enter holds the treasures you seek."

~JOSEPH CAMPBELL

I AM WAITING FOR MY CASKET to be delivered, though I have no idea where I will store it. My living room doesn't seem quite appropriate, but my rented storage unit is full. I should tell you how all this came about.

The small town where I live supports a business that makes one product and one product only—coffins, simple pine boxes with no nails. They are primarily used for traditional Jewish burials, but the business will sell to any interested customer. The reason for pine is that pine is a simple wood, and therefore confers no special status on one who is buried in it. Everyone is equal in leaving this earthly incarnation.

The synagogue where I served as rabbi had an annual auction to raise funds to help meet the operating budget. Everyone was asked to contribute in some way, large or small; the size of the contribution was less important than the act of participation. The two guys who had recently started a casket company generously donated a casket for the auction.

As part of the silent auction, all of the religious school

classrooms were filled with objects, or pages describing items and services. As is the usual custom in small, private auctions, participants bid by signing a bid sheet next to the object or description. Anyone who really wanted something could simply look at the last line on the list to see the current highest bid, and increase it.

As rabbi, I wanted all to feel their contributions were appreciated. I went from room to room bidding on anything that didn't have a bid. Not surprisingly, the casket had no bids. I entered my name alongside the minimum starting donation. When the time for bidding ended, I had a good deal on a casket.

I received a gift certificate with no expiration date. I could collect the casket whenever I wanted it. I hoped it would be a long time before I needed it, and I wasn't sure how I would get the casket if I died suddenly.

Five years passed. Then, ten years. During that time I was diagnosed with Parkinson's Disease. Since PD is considered a life-altering disease, not a life-threatening disease, I still felt no urgency to collect the casket.

More years passed and I realized I had no idea where I'd put the gift certificate. I looked in drawers and files, but with no success. Eventually, after about fifteen years, I surrendered to the fact that my good deal might not have been so good. Maybe I would never find the gift certificate, and it would be best to just write off the whole thing as a good deed.

One day, one of the men who started the casket company called me. He was the sole owner now and he saw his retirement around the corner. He wanted to make good on delivering all the caskets for which people had made arrangements. He didn't want anyone to be caught short in the time of need.

He said nothing about the gift certificate, just told me he wanted to deliver the casket to me sometime in the next few weeks. It would be disassembled and sealed in a plain cardboard box. I didn't intend to have a use for it before then, so we left it that he would call me in a few weeks.

Meanwhile I tried to find a home for the casket and struck out, which is when I got the idea to store it under my second-story front porch, where it would stay dry because of the overhang. At first I thought it would be morbid to have my casket so visible in all my comings and goings. Later the idea started to grow on me.

There is a Jewish practice of wearing a *kittel,* a white robe, during Passover and *Yom Kippur.* This is also the robe which one traditionally gets married in and the shroud in which one is traditionally buried. For me, seeing the *kittel* in the closet and wearing it on Passover and *Yom Kippur* is a visceral and powerful way of being mindful of my own mortality as part of the cycle of life. So, too, seeing the boxed and unassembled casket would serve as a daily reminder that my death is inevitable.

The day I had been anticipating arrived.

The plain cardboard box, about the size of a twin bed and about five inches thick, now lives under my porch, wrapped in a large brown tarp to keep it dry from any moisture the wind might blow its way. I see it whenever I enter or leave my home. It is a powerful reminder that my challenge is to live each day, each moment to its fullness.

The following *gatha*—one of a series of short verses intended to make one more mindful in daily life— that hung on my office door at the synagogue comes to mind whenever

I look at my pine box under the porch:
  "Let me respectfully remind you:

  Life and death are of supreme importance.
  Time swiftly passes by and opportunity is lost.
  Each of us should strive to awaken.
  Awaken! Take heed–do not squander your life."

Reflections

My body is tired with the constant shaking. The rigidity that sometimes happens to parts of my body can be quite painful, especially in the neck and shoulders. It is important that I find ways to restore and replenish the energy that the PD sucks out of me.

Meditation can be difficult to practice when one or more parts of my body are shaking, but it is still possible. My mind and body can be quiet, but not always when I want them to be. I practice watching how I react to my inability to quiet my body. The shaking is a physical incarnation of what Buddhism refers to as "monkey mind"—the constant mental chatter. Occasionally I find myself aware that I have stopped focusing on the tremors without even knowing it.

PD is a good teacher about surrender and not always needing to be in charge. Sometimes all I can do is ride out the tremors the way a surfer rides a cresting ocean wave. Sometimes I can just try to be like a tree, staying present without trying to do anything or make anything happen, just standing tall and allowing myself to move ever so slightly with the wind.

Sleep can be so delicious. I can't wait to crawl into bed around 8 p.m., or if I'm feeling really decadent, by 7:30. I awaken like clockwork at 4 a.m. I struggle to fall back asleep, and occasionally I'm successful.

One of the biggest changes I've made is how I respond to awakening in the middle of the night. I tried nearly all the techniques I could find, but the only thing that consistently worked was a highly addictive anti-anxiety pill. Not eager to get into a position that would inevitably take me into a toxic state of withdrawal hell, I worked very hard to stop taking it. Drugs can be life savers. They can also destroy lives.

Instead of fighting the inability to fall back asleep with more drugs, I've learned to surrender. If I'm going to be awake, I want to make the most of it. Why not turn sleeplessness into an opportunity! I started getting up and doing an hour of stretches, balancing work, and my own unofficial variation of yoga. I love having my exercises done for the day before taking my first round of meds at 6 a.m.

I am also learning how to use my time during the day more efficiently because everything takes longer and longer to do. What once was accomplished quickly, without much effort, now can take hours.

This can be a real test of the patience for the people around me, too. They don't get what is taking me so long, and I share their frustration with my sometimes-laborious process at completing simple tasks. It is made all the more difficult by how well I appear to be doing when my meds have kicked in. Sometimes one would hardly know I had PD. Those moments are few and far between but they do remind me of what my life used to be like.

CHAPTER 7

Bad Day on the River

"It always seems impossible until it's done."

~Nelson Mandela

Hardshell kayaking is, in my opinion, one of the greatest pleasures in life. Though it shares much in common with rafting and inflatable kayaking, it is significantly different. In a raft or an inflatable, one sits on top of the water. In a hardshell kayak the paddler is in, rather than on the river. That is the physical difference.

I had made a self-imposed vow three separate times in the last few years not to do anymore whitewater kayaking, but now, feeling the best I'd felt in more than fifteen years of living with PD, I decided to give it one more try. I had my eyes on paddling a stretch of the Klamath River that I knew like the back of my hand.

It seemed wise to work on a bomb-proof practice roll in a safe place before the rays of the summer sun beckoned me to the river, so on a surprisingly warm spring day, a friend and I went to a nearby lake. She spotted me in her kayak while I intentionally flipped my kayak. Then I tried to roll it right side up so that I'd be sitting once again atop the water, instead of fully submerged.

My expectations were low that warm spring day. I hadn't rolled in at least three years, maybe much longer. I didn't want to think about how long it had been. Utterly dumbfounded when, on my first attempt, I successfully rolled myself upright out of the water, I let out a big hoot. What an exquisite rush! Then on a dozen more attempts, I rolled upright on nine of them. I was not about to let it go to my head, but that felt pretty good to me. It led me to believe I could safely release myself from my vow to refrain from kayaking whitewater. There was no doubt about it, I still had some of my chops.

On a purely visceral level, it takes a certain amount of audacity and skill to be upside down in a turbulent, oxygen-deprived environment with rocks of all shapes and sizes ready to accost your skull at every moment on a potentially lethal obstacle course. At the same time you must orient yourself while upside down and unable to get any more oxygen. You need to wait for the right moment to do a six-step maneuver that, if executed correctly, will get you and your boat back upright in the water. The steps can't be rushed; each one is essential. It is an awesome feeling when it works.

It's breathtaking to watch it done well. Sometimes a paddler will choose to stay upside down for the entire length of a rapid, holding his breath, biding his time for upwards of two or three minutes till the water becomes less gnarly before rolling the craft back upright.

Following my initial exuberant success, the next week I found another friend to spot me. This practice session was going to be in a friend's swimming pool, and I felt optimistic. It didn't take long for my confidence-building experience of seven days before to come crashing down on me, much as a wave crashes over someone with his back turned to the surf.

I was unable to complete even one roll. What could I blame? I needed to find something to attribute this to. I left the pool believing this non-starter experience was due to being tired at the end of a busy day, but no amount of excuses could cover up the fact that I was not able to roll even once. If I experienced this kind of a day on the river, it could be very dangerous for myself and possibly others.

Which day was the anomaly? I wanted to wipe this most recent experience out of my mind-memory as well as my body-memory. I vowed I would not speak about it again. If I gave it no attention, surely it would gain no real power.

I knew enough about PD to know that my mind could play tricks on me. This was a big and potentially dangerous trick. I found myself hoping my inability to roll the second day would vanish with the same ease with which it had appeared.

It was proving to be difficult to find people to go kayaking with me. Some former paddling buddies had moved away. Others had ditched hardshell kayaks for a safer and less demanding type of boat, such as a raft, a cataraft floating on two inflatable tubes, or an inflatable kayak. Everyone seemed to have a decent reason for being unavailable. I tried my best not to make up stories and feel sorry for myself.

Finally, late one evening, I got my first positive response to my search for a boating buddy. My friend Randy didn't have a lot of experience, but she had a lot of heart and soul. Randy knew how much I loved kayaking and asked what my plans were. I texted back to her, "A very tame but fun section of the Klamath River." She replied, "I would be up for it, but only if we did rapids that are tame." We made plans for the next day, which couldn't come soon enough for me. Randy seemed as excited as I was to go out on the river.

We arrived at put-in and unloaded the boats and gear from Randy's car. I would be using one of my hardshell kayaks. Randy would be in a more comfortable and stable inflatable kayak.

It was fast approaching time when we would need to make a decision about how long we wanted to be out on the river. We had made arrangements with the campground host to shuttle our car to our take-out at the other end, but we had to tell the host where that would be. There was a take-out about four miles down the river from where we were now, and another take-out about five miles further beyond that, so we could do four miles or nine miles.

Randy thought that since we'd come all this way, we should do the longer run. I wasn't going to argue. I mentioned that the most challenging two rapids would be near the end of the longer run, but while I wouldn't really call them tame, I had never felt real danger there in the many times I had previously been down this section of the river. Was I honoring my commitment to Randy to only do "tame" sections of the river? Was I morphing my definition of tame? Had I made an agreement with Randy that I wasn't living up to? I still ponder those questions.

More than any concern about the size of the rapids on this section of the river, I wondered about my stamina. As I was the experienced one, I didn't want to alarm her with my fears, worries, or concerns. Despite my secret misgivings, we opted for the longer run. PD has sometimes let me fool myself into making questionable choices. I don't like to admit that I am, in some ways, a shadow of my former self, but if I'm honest with myself, I believe it to be true. Nonetheless I want to maintain the illusion, when possible, that the effects of the disease are not as great as they indeed are. Often the results of this kind of hubris don't catch up to me till long after my precipitous behavior, but this time I didn't have long to wait.

At some point in the first four miles, I flipped my kayak over. Unintentionally. I set up for a roll, and wonder of wonders, this bizarre series of maneuvers worked. I was back above the water, my spray skirt was still attached to my boat, and I didn't have to swim or retrieve an empty boat. Randy thought I flipped on purpose.

It was after this that I had the first inkling of a nagging voice I didn't want to hear—that the shorter run would have been enough. Everything was going well. Until it wasn't. Around mile six, fatigue began to take charge and the voices in my head became bolder. You've bitten off more than you can chew. Better cop to the mistakes you've made before it's too late. It might already be too late.

I flipped a second time in a place that had never been trouble before. After three attempts to roll, I pulled my spray skirt off the cockpit of my boat and, eager for oxygen, swam toward the surface of the river.

The two "bigger" rapids now loomed large in my mind. It was time to take my meds and the timing wasn't good—it would take about an hour before I could count on the meds to kick in. If it were earlier in the day we could have pulled over to the side of the river to hang out and wait for that to happen, but unless we were willing to be on the river at night—which I most definitely wanted to avoid—we didn't have an hour to wait. I paddled over to the edge of the river, opened a small dry bag, and took my meds.

At the same time, I balanced on a rock and summoned what little strength I had left to drain the boat, which has to be done periodically. It takes an enormous amount of energy to get water out of a kayak. Water is very heavy and it's difficult to find an optimal position for lifting up the boat, so maintaining balance and not slipping or falling onto a rock and cracking your head open is always a concern. I completed the operation, but it drained much of my remaining energy.

Randy and I both made it through the first of the two "un-tame" rapids. It wasn't pretty, but we both stayed in our boats. We had one more significant rapid to get through. As we approached it, the sound of the river got exponentially louder.

I pointed out to Randy a good place to enter the rapid. "You see that pyramid rock sticking out of the water? You want to go just to the right of that. It's about a three- or four-foot drop. Keep the front of your boat pointed forward as you enter the rapid.

"When you get to the bottom of the falls, the water gets pretty funky so don't think you can relax. The water will try to push you into some large boulders. Paddle hard and try to move toward the center of the river, but watch out for a large hole that will try to suck you into its vortex. One last thing—remember to look where you want to go, not where you don't want to go." That was a lot of information—and warnings—for Randy, a relative newbie, to digest.

I went first over the drop. There was less room to maneuver than I remembered. I quickly eddied out of the main flow of the river and into calmer water, where I could watch Randy come through the small keyhole at the top of the waterfall. I looked up in time to see her enter the keyhole and flip over in the inflatable kayak, right at the top of the falls.

It was not a good place to flip. A leg or a foot could easily be entrapped by a rock.

Randy's vest did its job, and her head popped up out of the water to get her some needed air, along with a mouthful of unneeded river water. She tried to swim over to me but couldn't make it. The strong flow of the river had other plans for her and dragged her quickly downstream without a boat. I looked around to see if I could spot her inflatable. I saw it caught in a not-too-distant eddy.

Randy had now completely disappeared from my view. She would need her boat to go any further. It was up to me to get it to her. There was no one else around who was going to do it. I hoped a rush of adrenalin would support what I needed to do. I safely paddled over to Randy's boat and then tried to push it out of the eddy, but the current and the wind blew it further up river. I tried again and again. Nothing I did was making any noticeable difference.

I saw a tie-down strap that was holding an air pump in the back of Randy's boat. I figured if we lost the air pump but got the boat out, that would be a good trade. I affixed the tie-down strap to her boat and then to mine. But no matter what I tried, I could not break through the eddy line and get her boat free.

By this point I was running on empty. I was surprised to see, or at least I thought I was seeing, Randy making her way up on the boulders that lined the right bank of the river. She had her paddle with her. I was impressed by her tenacity and determination. Was I hallucinating? What was being demanded of her was neither safe nor easy, but she was rising to the task.

Randy made her way over to me and her boat. I tried to hold her boat steady as she climbed from a fallen log down into it. Before situating herself in her boat, she astutely noticed that I no longer had my paddle in my hands, and asked about it.

"I don't know what happened to it." I didn't seem to care much. "I can do without it. I don't need it." Randy and I looked directly into each other's eyes. We didn't have to say anything. We both realized I was no longer thinking clearly.

Randy had seen me holding my paddle only minutes before and wasn't going to take "I don't know what happened to it" as the final answer. She intuitively reached under the log she had used to climb into her boat and pulled out my paddle. Randy was either becoming a magician or a miracle worker. I was in too much of an altered state to be impressed.

I knew we had to get out of the eddy and continue down river. The eddy line was strong going upriver and the main current was strong going down river. I paddled my way out of the eddy and in a split second, found myself upside down in the far-from-tame water. I knew I would not be able to do a successful roll so I didn't even try.

I pulled off my spray skirt to free myself from the boat. I needed oxygen—I hadn't taken a big enough breath to stay under water for very long—and made a beeline for the surface. As I gulped in deep breaths of air, my boat suddenly took off down river without me. I tried to catch it but stopped just short of getting caught in the main current, which surely would have taken me to places I didn't wish to go. For the time being, I was somewhat safe in the small eddy that had found me.

Randy looked at me. I looked at her. She looked clearly confused. Then these words came out of her mouth, "Do I stay with you or go after your boat?" There was no way she was going to get over to where I was in her boat. I pointed for her to go down river.

Randy made her way down the river, and where the river made a bend to the right, she disappeared from my view. I had no way of knowing if she was trying to rescue my boat, had flipped again herself, or what new situation she was encountering. I tried calling out to her, but that proved futile. The sound of the river drowned out all other sounds. Both of us were on our own.

Darkness was fast approaching and I was no longer seeing the river as a friendly place. I wanted to get out. It was as if the river had suddenly become shark infested. The only safe place for me at that moment was to be on solid ground. That proved to be more difficult than I ever could have imagined.

The entire bank along the river's edge where I stood half in and half out of the water was covered as far as the eye could see by the largest, most gnarly, inhospitable and uninviting jungle of blackberry bushes I had ever seen. The branches were about an inch thick, too thin to walk on, but too thick to be pushed aside. The seemingly infinite number of thorns were poised and waiting for action, eager to show their superiority to barbed wire.

There was no way to get safely onto land without dealing with those warrior plants. It still looked better to me than entering the river with no boat in the middle of a big rapid. I imagined the river would swallow me up and spit me out into a feeding frenzy of hungry sharks. The blackberry brambles would not be as dramatic as the sharks, but would draw my blood just as efficiently. They were ready and waiting, tall and resilient, for someone foolish enough to enter their lair.

I began first by trying to muscle my way through them. Anyone watching would surely have laughed. It is ridiculous to think that anyone could muscle through blackberry brambles. The only choice I had was to climb up and over the top of each one. Each attempt to step on and then over a blackberry bush had the same torturous outcome.

I fell through the twisted limbs. My downward movement suddenly stopped just as my toes barely touched the ground. As I dangled there, the thorns dug deeper into my flesh. To take the next step, I had to lift myself up off the very same thorns that had just embedded themselves in me. I moved forward another foot, trying not to fall through into the bush, but I couldn't stop myself. I fell into the brambles again. I was getting nowhere in a hurry.

It was during one of my "hanging rest stops" that a new possibility occurred to me: I was in rattlesnake country. There would be no way I could make a fast exit were I to encounter one. I wondered if my fresh blood would attract or repel them. I imagined an obituary in the newspaper reading something like: "Man Bloodied by Blackberry Bushes, Finished off by Rattlesnake, Buried in Plain Pine Coffin."

I was aware that night was falling. I couldn't think of a worse place to sleep than on a bed of nails, so I kept trying to move forward, getting more and more panicked with every movement. Fortunately at that point my meds started to kick in. I heard a voice I thought I recognized in the distance. Could it really be Randy? Then I saw her above me, on solid ground. I was so relieved she was okay. I tried to stand up to call out to her, but I could not remain upright for even a second. Again I fell through the branches. More thorns. More blood. I called out to her, waving my bloody but happy-to-be-seen arms.

Randy had returned with another woman to help her, and it was she who spotted me first. There was quite a distance of steep terrain separating us. The woman disappeared for a few minutes and returned carrying two large thick blue tarps. She shook out one of them until it caught some air and came to rest on top of the blackberry bushes. Then she did the same with the second tarp, narrowing the distance between us. Playing some kind of leapfrog game, she and Randy moved ever closer to me.

I was too weak and tired to get up on my own, so I remained prone, waiting and watching. The two women worked well together and finally got to me. Using the two blue tarps, we clumsily leap-frogged together over the entire width of the brambles and came out on a dirt road.

I saw what looked to be a slightly broken lawn chair and practically fell into it from exhaustion. The weathered canvas of the seat didn't look like it would hold many more sits and the large ripping sound that accompanied my sitting did more than suggest that this was the last time anyone would be sitting in this chair. I asked this unexpectedly generous woman if she had any drinking water. She walked away and came back a few minutes later with three bottles of water, which I downed in quick succession.

Darkness was coming on quickly. These two women, who had successfully retrieved me, now left me to recover and took it upon themselves to retrieve the boats and get them to a place that was car accessible. As soon as they left I started pulling thorns out of my river sandals, my pants, my feet, my lower legs, and my arms. I was covered in dried and fresh blood.

While the two women were gone (I had decided they surely must both be angels), a man sauntered down the dirt road adorned in slacks and a crisp blue and white pinstriped jacket and tie. He was dressed for another place and time. I thought I was hallucinating.

When he saw the two women lifting an inflatable kayak over their heads in the distance, he asked if I would give his "better half" a message that he was home, and I said I gladly would. When the women returned and I'd relayed the message, she drove us down to the takeout where Randy's car had been parked earlier in the day. Randy and I switched to her car and followed the mystery woman to the place where they had left the boats. It wasn't until we got the boats loaded onto the roof of Randy's car, and the wet and smelly gear into a mesh bag and onto the rear seat, that I began to feel better.

Randy and I expressed our abundant gratitude to this angel of a woman and drove away into the proverbial sunset, the dropping orb lighting the sky with bright shades of orange, red, and deep blue light. The entryway to heaven probably looks something like this.

We drove home in awe and mostly in silence. We acknowledged that there was still one piece of gratitude we had not yet expressed. It was to the river. I had said a few days earlier that the short and longer runs were tame parts of the river, but only the shorter section was truly tame for us that day.

I'd made errors in judgment and the river had nearly swallowed us both. It could easily have taken one or both of our lives, but it didn't. It had shown us that being strong and powerful doesn't prevent the river from also being grace-filled and forgiving.

I have heard stories of expert kayakers disappearing on what to them was surely a "tame" section of river. We all make errors in judgement, not just on the river, but any and everywhere. When I go on the river with PD I'm taking more risks than someone without PD, despite my skill and experience. But my errors in judgement, especially when others are involved, also make it more challenging to recover safely.

To say that it had been a bad day on the river is not speaking the deeper truth. It was not a bad day on the river. I had forgotten for a period of time about my PD. I had kayaked some thrilling waves. I had plunged into some big holes and had come out on the opposite side still upright in my boat. The river had been forgiving and so had Randy. I had had a series of experiences I will never forget, and bonded with Randy in a way that has made us lifelong friends. And through all this I had continued learning about life and living with PD. It had been a good day…a good day on the river.

~

Reflections

The final reflections in this book are things I've never wanted to deal with. It's no accident that they come toward the end. They are reminders that no matter how good I'm feeling, those feelings can change at a moment's notice. I must not shut my eyes to some tough realities that come with PD.

Compulsions may accompany drugs used for treating PD. Although they are often referred to as "side effects," they have the ability to become the main show quickly, with little warning and little time to deflect them. My neurologist spoke to me about compulsive behaviors that could easily become an addiction. I asked him rather casually, "Like what behavior?" He gave me the examples of binge buying with credit cards and compulsive gambling. I asked if it was a compulsion to stay up nearly every night until the wee hours of the morning working on my photography. I do my best work late at night when everything's still and quiet, and I like being able to hear myself think.

He said that was a good example, but that it didn't feel like it was a danger to myself or others. I agreed and added that it might be a bigger danger to myself and others if I had to give up my photography, even if I am compulsive about it. My neurologist concurred and asked me to tell him if I noticed any new compulsions.

I later became aware that I was engaging in more compulsive behavior than I'd realized. Though I didn't see it as compulsive at the time, I had gotten into looking on the

Internet for the perfect messenger bag, the perfect day pack, and the perfect carry-on luggage. Before I knew it, I had quite a collection going. People started teasing me about it when I arrived at work every few weeks with what I claimed was an even better perfect bag. I still didn't catch on that I was engaging in compulsive behavior, or that it was related to the PD meds I was taking.

I came across a small article in a newspaper about medical evidence linking a more recently approved PD drug I was taking to a compulsion that I hadn't heard of before: sexually reckless behavior. The article gave an example of a man who had seen seventy prostitutes in the past year. I wasn't experiencing that kind of behavior, so I still didn't link it to things that were happening in my own life—my marriage was coming apart and I had become involved with another woman. I'm not sure which came first, but the situation was making my life untenable and unhealthy. I vacillated between my desire to heal my marriage and my desire to flee all that had changed in my life in favor of sex and romance.

At a neurology appointment I learned that my intense confusion could be connected to a side effect of a drug I had been taking. My neurologist apologized for not making me aware of this possibility sooner, and advised me to get off the drug and see how I was without it. He explained it would take about three months to get the drug fully out of my system.

I weaned myself off the drug. My marriage ended. I found myself outside the gates of Paradise with no way back in. It took me a number of years to find myself again.

Depression comes with the territory. It is hard not to feel down for short and sometimes long periods of time. One problem I've had with depression isn't so much with the depression itself, but with getting off the addictive prescription meds I formerly used to treat depression. It is very difficult to say no to a drug that can be effective in as little as thirty minutes. The problem I faced was that the relief the drugs were bringing to me in my depression brought with them an even tougher reality.

Depression is one of the trickier areas to navigate. When I expect a few bumps and bruises, I'm not so caught by surprise. I have, through watching my own reactions, developed a list of activities that almost always help me get out of a funk. Many of these are universally enjoyed, but being able to experience them through or in spite of my disability seems to intensify my pleasure. Remember, just a few years ago I thought I'd be spending the rest of my life in a wheelchair.

- *Music.* Listening, finding new music that resonates, dancing to great music.
- *Movement in nature.* Hiking, walking on a beach, planting flower bulbs, taking care of a garden, running, climbing a tree.
- *Going inward.* Meditating, reading a new poem or a profound spiritual book.
- *Creativity.* Taking photographs, singing songs.
- *Food.* A nourishing meal, ice cream, a good cup of joe, a warm donut.
- *Simple pleasures.* Making a great fire with only one match, taking a bath, soaking in a hot tub under a

starry sky, loud and close thunder and lighting, a windy day, bright autumn leaves, a good laugh, tears of joy.

- *Appreciation.* A beautiful full moon, snow falling, rainbows, spring flowers, fragrant roses, a good night's sleep, remembering a great dream.
- Self-care and caring for others. Getting or giving a massage, playing with a friendly dog or scratching a purring cat.
- *Relationship.* Holding hands and walking with someone I love, making love, morning cuddles and nighttime snuggles.

Suicide is an act of desperation, and I don't know anyone who has PD who hasn't considered it.

For five months I took weekly hikes with a woman who was as committed to fighting her version of PD as I am to mine. She stuck with her program. She took her meds at precisely the "right" time and didn't take them within an hour and a half of eating protein. And she was able to keep up with the fast pace that served best to subdue the effects of my PD.

Then she took her life. I think my friend saw herself and PD as separate entities. She imagined the PD was moving its forces in to defeat her. It had become too difficult and she saw no hope on the horizon, so death looked like the only way out. It is, in fact, the only way out, but she checked out way ahead of check-out time.

I had listened well to what she was saying on our hikes, but I had no idea that she would actually take her life two weeks after first mentioning it. Her death nearly delivered a knock-out punch. Who was I trying to fool? Did I think that all this exercise could actually make a positive difference in my life? Was I delaying the inevitable? Was she more in touch with her feelings than I was? I was clear that I was not ready to give up.

What makes PD so difficult is not just the idea of living with the disease, or the depression that can be an integral part of the illness, it is also the exhaustion. It is a desire for the incessant shaking, both inside and out, to stop. A weariness sets in as the experience of peace and quiet recedes to a distant memory.

PD is a remorseless thief that has stolen a long list of things from me. First and foremost is my independence, which is disappearing right before my eyes and is linked to everything else I have lost. My spontaneous energy is gone and everything is a big effort. Things that once were simple, like putting a key in a door lock, can take me what seems like forever. I need shoes without laces because tying them is so difficult.

My dignity is often among the missing. In a public restroom I feel self-conscious that other men might think I'm jerking off because the tremor makes things look that way. It is humiliating to freeze in a doorway while everyone wants to help me, but no one really knows what to do. It is frustrating for all concerned when the people I love most cannot hear or understand me, over and over and over again.

During times of constant freezes, I pee into a bottle at the edge of my bed because the freezes prevent me from getting to the toilet in time (This has thankfully passed as have the constant freezes.)

My hand tremors wake me in the middle of the night, and make me anxious that the sound of my shaking hand against the sheets will disturb my sweetheart. Adherence to a rigid three- and four-hour medication schedule every day is essential, month after month, year after year if I want to count on any consistent and regular kind of activity schedule. It's not one of these things that wears me down and prompts me to think about checking out. It is dealing with all of these things for sixteen years.

After my friend died it took about six weeks for me to get the monkey off my shoulder and out of my daily life. This tormenting creature took marching orders directly from the PD. I knew a part of me was creating this creature. He challenged and belittled all my attempts to better myself or to contain the negative effects of this progressive and degenerative neurological disease.

As time passed, I saw that I was doing better than I'd realized and made a very conscious decision to keep my focus on that. But I remain quite aware that suicide is a dangerous manifestation of PD and it's important to take it seriously. I have known three people with PD who have taken their own lives.

CHAPTER 8

Heaven on Earth

SOMETIMES GETTING THROUGH A DAY with PD is living hell. Some days it is a big nuisance. Other days have lovely, even beautiful moments. I never know what to expect and I try to stay open to whatever appears. I try to remember that, like life and the rivers I love, living with PD is neither good nor bad. Living with PD is just living with PD, and any pain or suffering that comes with it is just the pain and suffering that comes with it. Rather than give up, I continually work at surrendering to what is.

It does no good to hide from PD. There is more power in acknowledging what it is doing to me at any given time. At first I thought I could deny everything, that the PD was all in my head. If I took it out of my head, it followed that it wouldn't affect my life. I came to see the fallacy in that belief. Now I admit to myself how I am affected by my illness. By not denying the reality of PD, I am better able to cope with it.

If there is a silver lining it is that I am learning not to hide, which is something I've struggled with throughout my life. PD's way of operating is to make itself visible. It is turning out to be a great teacher.

I remember when Michael J. Fox's book *Lucky Man* first came out in 2002. I was eager to learn how he was coping with the disease. He put a quote on the back cover that may have been more powerful to me than anything I read in the text: "The ten years since my diagnosis have been the best ten years of my life, and I consider myself a lucky man."

At that time I wasn't ready to hear such treason. I threw the book across the room. But I needed to wake up to the challenges that awaited me. These days I find myself saying nearly the same thing.

I sold my cataraft five years ago. I gave away my sit-on-top kayak two years ago. About a month ago I gifted my two hardshell kayaks to friends. That left me with one boat—a previously little used high-end inflatable kayak.

It had been two years since I'd last used that kayak. With much improvement in my health and encouragement from my sweetheart, yesterday I felt emboldened to do a day trip with river buddies who understand my challenges and limitations. It was an auspicious day, a full moon, Friday the thirteenth. The white water was minimal Class I and I navigated it easily, and while it wasn't the rush I get from big water, nevertheless I was on the river.

Sometimes even beliefs I 'know' are true need to be reconsidered and changed. I didn't think I belonged on the river anymore. With a big smile on my face, I realized I was wrong. For with hard work, determination, and the help of loving friends, I can still paddle a kayak in a river I love, surrounded by people I love. This gets me pretty close to experiencing heaven on earth. I am a lucky man.

~

Index of Reflections

Acknowledgments

Many people have contributed in many ways to bringing this book into your hands.

Let me begin with my parents—Richard and Esther. Throughout my life they have always been there for me. My deepest gratitude to them both.

Fayegail Mandell Bisaccia has been editor, close friend, and colleague for nearly twenty-five years. She was my rabbinic assistant for approximately fourteen years, and she read, critiqued, and improved almost everything I wrote. That is certainly the case with this book. Her advice and wisdom are on every page. She knows me well and we share a unique vulnerability and honesty. We have shed many tears together—not only tears of sadness, but also tears of joy—and shared many belly laughs.

Dr. Leonard Felder is my guru for writing non-fiction books. He is the author of many books, and from day one has been an encouraging guide, inspiration, and mentor for me in writing and publishing this book. He has thanked me in his books for my contributions, and I am thrilled that it is my turn to thank him.

Libba Coker was my sweetheart for much of the writing of this book. We decided to uncouple shortly before the Covid-19 pandemic began. She has taught me much about myself as she has revealed things to me about her own life. She models for me what it means to be an engaged Buddhist, and has helped me to better understand what it might mean for me to be an engaged Jewish Buddhist. Her generosity is unparalleled.

I have quite a list of river friends. Some have taught

me new paddling skills. Others have helped me by offering suggestions on ways I might improve my roll. Others have actually helped rescue me when I have taken on more white water than I could safely manage. These "river buddies" include Teal Kinamun, Mimi Margulies, Jonnie Dale Leiberman, Gary Berlant, Jimbo, Larry Davis, Peter Dratch, and Dr. Craig Mather.

I am also grateful to Teal and Mimi, as well as other friends and colleagues, for reading an early draft of this book and giving me wonderfully helpful feedback. Lance Bisaccia, Shifra Glaser, and Avara Yaron, also gave me valuable thoughts and notes after reading an early draft. Thanks to all of you.

It has been nearly two years since Ruth Resch was in this earthly space and time. She was present for this book's first flowerings, giving me daily encouragement to write my story and let go of any shame I carried. She helped me turn a number of corners at major intersections in my life.

Various healers I have worked with have made a huge difference in my healing and my improved health. I particularly thank Sheila Filan for the last eight years of weekly Feldenkrais work. Thanks, also, to Steve Glaser for venturing deep into his understanding of Asian Medicine in order to help me. Thanks to Karen Pederson for helping me find the courage to move my body in dance. And thank you to Dr. Cory Tichauer, N.D., for his wisdom, care, and depth of knowledge. He has led me to believe in the efficacy of Functional Medicine.

I also wish to thank my neurologists, Dr. Michael Narus, Dr. Jay Nutt, Dr. Neal Hermanowicz, Dr. Michael Presti, and Dr. Pawani Sachar for listening to me and choosing with me how best to help me, based on my needs and intentions.

Thank you, also, to all the other Western healers, doctors, nurses, and medical assistants who so much want to help me, and other folks like me, deal with a life-altering disease.

There are three more individuals I wish to thank and acknowledge: Sharon Dvora, with whom I traveled to Bali, accepted me and loved me despite my shortcomings. Carol Sunahara, who drove me half an hour each way every week to take part in a life-changing exercise class for people with PD. And finally, thanks to Curly Dykstra, who turned an empty exercise room into a noisy, sweaty place of hope, health, and change for people with PD. I am doing as well as I am, in large part, because Curly had a vision and found a path to make it happen.

About the Author

Marc Sirinsky served as rabbi to a congregation in Ashland, Oregon for nearly twenty five years. Midway through those years he learned he had Parkinson's Disease. Although he rarely kayaks these days, he has continued other activities that bring him joy—traveling, hiking, photographing, teaching, and listening to all kinds of music. Prior to becoming a rabbi, Marc was an award winning writer/director for theatre, TV, and film. He is the proud father of a wonderful daughter and two lively and lovely grandchildren.

www.ingramcontent.com/pod-product-compliance
Ingram Content Group UK Ltd.
Pitfield, Milton Keynes, MK11 3LW, UK
UKHW022006190726
13853UKWH00004B/1764

9 798985 127102